Ida M. White

Brokenness TO BEAUTIFUL

Brokenness TO BEAUTIFUL

Published by Krystal Lee Enterprises (KLE Publishing)
Copyright © 2024 by Ida M. White
All rights reserved. Please send comments and questions:
Krystal Lee Enterprises
770-240-0089 Ext. 1
sales@KLEPub.com
To Reach the Author:
Phone: 407-910-4972
Email: ida.b.white@gmail.com
Web: DrIdaMWhite.com
Social Media All Channels:

Printed in the United States of America.
All rights reserved. No part of this book may be reproduced or transmitted in any form or by any means, electronic or mechanical, including photocopying, recording, or any information storage and retrieval system without written permission of the publisher except for brief quotations used in reviews, written specifically for inclusion in a newspaper, blog, magazine, or academic paper.

ISBN: 978-1-945066-71-9

Welcome to all

    Thanks so much for choosing my book and sharing my life's journey. God forbid, if it seems like a history book–although my life story began 89 years ago (in New York City) amidst many settings that may be unfamiliar to you. Yet, as I weave through the intricacies of my life, I know that life from those days always came with some story. It was a time of the radio, 78 rpm records, 10-inch and 12-inch TVs, frozen foods, supermarkets were emerging, and the party line–rotary telephones emerged if you were lucky enough to have one.

    In today's world, telephones fit in the palm of your hand and send messages instantly. Music is available instantly. Travel is not instant but everywhere. Thousands of vastly improved hi-tech lifestyles have moved us from the slow to the right now. The idea of life and living is so advanced; it's on another level.

    The significant part is that throughout my almost 90 years, I have had and still have the opportunity to use and wade through all these technologies. So, just for the heck of it, let me leave you with this question: " Why did the smartphone go to school? Because it wanted to be smart from the start and not like its great grandparent, the rotary phone, which always needed someone to dial things in." Chuckles and giggles.

Brokenness to Beautiful

Table of Contents

Prologue	7
Chapter One	13
Chapter Two	21
Chapter Three	43
Chapter Four	63
Chapter Five	75
Chapter Six	87
Chapter Seven	95
Epilogue	121
About the Author	125

Prologue

Naming the beautiful brown baby girl after her paternal grandmother, Ida, was an act of love, devotion, and respect that her father smiled about as he held her shortly after her birth. He suspected she would be tall, just like his mother Ida. As she started bawling for nursing, he grew sad for a moment. He prayed that she would have a wonderful, happy life. As her mother cuddled her for nursing, she was proud of her little Ida. She wanted her to have her mother's name, Charlotte, but she agreed with Edward on Ida.

She prayed that Ida would get a good education and be solid and intelligent like her mother, Charlotte. She hoped she would not have to work hard and get little money. The Depression was almost over, it seemed. She watched Edward; he seemed so happy at being a father, but she and him were not going to make it. He wanted her to live in S.C., Florence. That could never be. She had left there forever—the miseries of just trying to exist, and the exhaustion of farm life.

Living in Florence would mean working like a dog. No, this was not for her. Look what his mom, Ida

(Mamay), went through. Look how his Father died and why. No, no. Idamay would be safer in New York City she thought. God would help her to be a good mother. Edward's family would help her out so she could return to working in a few months. She would find a job.

Mamay was coming up from South Carolina in 3 months. She promised to take care of her new grand baby and her other grandson. She could not wait to meet this woman who she had heard about. However, she had only heard the whispers about her from Edward's distant family and friends in secret.

They all were good people, though, and Edward's brother and his wife, Genia, always had a happy house full of people. Curtis loved to sing. They were friends and knew top singing groups like the Mills Brothers and The Ink Spots, and Maggie liked going to their home.

They were the superintendents of the house where she was going to move. They were excited about her being pregnant. Wait until they see Idamay Edward thought. **Edward wanted to take me to live in South Carolina, but that's out of the question.**

Maggie's thoughts returned to Mamay as Ida slept in her father's arms.

Mamay had six sons born in the Florence County area of South Carolina; Edward was the youngest, born in 1901. Patrick Brown was his father. Patrick was a God-fearing man; he was happy to marry Mamay and have a family of children. He had grown up in Florence County and wanted to do the right thing to be safe and

Prologue

keep his family safe.

To keep his Ida safe, she was so beautiful to him. She cooked everything he loved from the garden. She could milk a cow expertly, and once he made the butter for her biscuits, it would all melt in your mouth. Everything seemed like it was going to be perfect. Ida was pregnant, they were going to have their first child… and then "it" happened in the middle of the night. They were driven out of their home by three hooded tormentors.

Everything they owned was broken up, and they started setting the little cabin ablaze. For some reason, they didn't, and they rode off, leaving Ida and Patrick huddled together, terrified for fear they would return. They did not return, yet there was a deep-rooted fear of the future.

But my grandmother and grandfather dropped to their knees and prayed, thanking God for retaining their lives by the power of God. They were asking and praying to God for his care. Patrick asked to be a strong man so he could protect his family.

The crooked path of injustices against my grandparents was to straighten out without being made straight. To remain safe in that festering hole on their own was impossible; they were doomed. The story of this Brown family begins that night when, on the next day, Patrick protects himself and his family by entering himself and his wife Ida into a lifetime relationship with a wealthy white farmer and sharecropper.

It would appear that Ida would have children for

her husband and children for the white farmer. When it was completed many years later, by 1902, Ida had borne six living, healthy sons: three for Patrick and three for the wealthy white sharecropper. All the sons bore the name Brown and were raised by Patrick.

By the time Patrick was 50, he had passed away, leaving his beloved Ida alone with sons who were a part of the "shackles" of Ida and Patrick's past. Ida had a spirit of resilience. She was the embodiment of strength as she endured the struggles brought about by her apparent humiliation, as well as the scars that would always be a part of her life and her son's lives.

The Brown sons left Florence County, SC, except Sam (half white) and Edward, full black. Sam inherited his father's sense of business. As a highly respected businessman, He and Edward maintained an underground protection for the hopeless victims of racism. However, the other first names bore the mark of the white sharecropper.

Wherever they were and wherever the sons and their families went, their hearts beat to the rhythm of their black heritage. However, some of the second generation's grandchildren could not reconcile and became alcoholics, struggling with social norms and shame. Some found it challenging to understand and forgive Mamay.

She lived with their hostility and faced some incredibly difficult challenges of some judgmental and unforgiving hearts of those who should have understood. In 1941, her son Edward, my father, passed in his mother's arms. In her older years, she learned to pray a lot and

Prologue

sensed God's spirit for the positive elements of her life.

She had then, I suspect, whispered in granddaughter Ida's ears all of her hopes and dreams for her. She had often prayed I'm sure that Ida would lead a powerful and happy life, that she would be strong and resilient. She must have wished for her a life that would be happy, joyous, and beautiful.

In Florence, South Carolina, her life had begun to turn around, and she was no longer concerned about those who were judgmental. About 12 years ago, my cousin on my mom's side told me she had lived near my grandmother Ida in Florence, SC; she had her own home then. My cousin said that she was a nice older lady.

(That short comment was so important to me) I now recognize that her silent strength and inner beauty mirrored the stories of biblical heroines and hundreds, if not thousands, of others. In other words, they were strong women whose lives were not lives of choice but their destiny.

My father, Edward, died in 1941. Years later, at different times, my grandma Ida and my Uncle Sam were all three put to their resting place in the cemetery of the wealthy sharecropper in Florence County, SC. This is the resting place where the ideals of individuals still remain divided by a person's color and class.

My grandmother's legacy to me is her enduring power of the human spirit, which I have waited 88 years to acknowledge. I once had a lovely picture of her. Now, though, even without a picture of her face, she is in my heart. She was always walking with me and talking to me, even at my young age, sharing with me her concerns for herself in her days of torment and for me as I struggled to survive as a single, only child as well.

Chapter One

Harlem

There is a 3D picture that comes to mind of my life as a very young Ida Lewis living in Harlem. The central neighborhood for African Americans in the late 1930s coming out of the Great Depression, but in my visual, the picture represents the beginning of life for me, Ida May Lewis. I don't remember being a baby, the crawling baby, or the first-step baby. Yet, I remember that playground; I had emerged from there.

As I got to be around four years old, or even before, sliding at any age on the slide board was fun. Being on the swing was super fun. As I got older, it was still an enjoyable place for me to go. When there was no school, on the weekends, or on holidays, that's where you could find me, especially at the age of five. It was the playground on the corner of 131st St. and 5th Ave!

That playground had everything a child could want. It had monkey bars, swings and slides, a seesaw, and lots of room to run, jump, and have fun. If you went to the playground, you were sure to find some of your friends there. Yes, that playground was filled with so many good memories. There were other opportunities surrounding the playground for more happiness for us as children.

I remember there was a candy store on one side of the street. In the summertime, you could get delicious snow cones for two cents from little shaved ice trucks on baby carriage wheels. At my age, I was not allowed to go to the playground by myself, and there was always an older child around the apartment area who would be happy for a candy bar from my mother or godmother to take me or a group of us to the playground.

Summertime would often bring about the opening of the fire hydrants by the firemen in the nearby area. We then had the opportunity to put on a bathing suit, run up and down around the fire hydrant, and enjoy ourselves on sweltering summer days. And, of course, it was not unusual for the iceman to be cutting a block of ice to carry to someone's apartment, and guess what? It would not be a surprise if the iceman gave you a piece of ice that had spiked off the block. That was always fun!

As I relate the day-to-day structure throughout the first part of my life, I often remember those days visually, in memory, or conversation as I reflected over the years. I used to have many albums of Kodak camera pictures from my infancy and the early years of my mother holding me. Every photo of me and my family, including certificates, diplomas, and some report cards, were destroyed in recent years.

More on that later. So, I ask you to please trust

Chapter One

my memory for my accuracy as best as possible. I've been blessed to have a good memory, and I will share it as accurately as possible.

My commentary on my thoughts and feelings is part of what it was like for me to live day-to-day in my little world. My hope, joy, pain, and sorrow are very personal. At 65, I would not have shared my life this way, yet, at my age of 89, I feel encouraged to share.

My mother, Ms. Maggie, was known to most people when I began to understand her. She worked often and frequently, as I recall growing up. My "fairy" godmother and daycare teacher, Ms. Arsula, was my mother's very good friend, with whom I spent most of my early years like some other neighborhood kids.

She was a wonderful Christian lady who took me to church every Sunday and provided the foundation for what I like to eat and drink for these 89 years of my life. I salute her now for the love she always showed me. I loved her dearly and still do.

We all lived in the same apartment, and it was an apartment with lots of space. My aunt, who was married to my uncle Curtis and who was the superintendent of the building, lived downstairs in the basement. They were also my caregivers. The block's neighbors often sat outside the building in the terrace area, chatting with each other until it was time for the soap operas. I can really see them now. Not faces but the energy from their conversations as well as their laughter.

Nearby was 125th St. It was the shopping Mecca

for Harlem residents. It was where the movie theaters were. It had the Apollo, and if you went all the way down 125th St., you could see a variety of shops, vegetable stands, bakeries, and everything that you could ever want. There were bookstores, book stands, different types of restaurants, and small cafes.

I remember there was the famous department stores that I knew of even at the age of 4. Blumstein's Dept. Store and Woolworth, a national shoe store, were there. The first time I ever saw pizza was on 125th St.

Harlem was the place that I assumed I would see every day of my life. I wasn't aware of anything bad about it or anything that wasn't good for everyone who knew and lived. And, in the area where I lived in late afternoons, whether it was a weekday or a Sunday, you could always hear the radio. The radio commentaries or the sound of a radio show, or the soap operas, daily and on many afternoons, Saturdays and Sundays were sports. There were church services on Sunday mornings, and it was Jack Benny on Sunday evenings.

As a child, life was fun, and I wasn't aware of danger. My knowledge of things came about as a result of hearing everything mentioned and spoken of by the adults I lived around. Yet, let me not get too far ahead of myself. My uncle and his family stayed close in contact with me. He had two nearly grown sons and a daughter who was a teenager. He also helped my mother out by looking after me when it was necessary.

My mother had two friends who were roommates who lived in the same apartment house right next door.

Chapter One

They watched out for me also. I had a play brother, JR, who was two years older than me, and Aletha was like a big sister to me. Talk about how "it takes a village to raise a child!" It was perfectly set up for a complete unhinged success in child rearing, even in Harlem!

I started school when I was four years old because I could read, and it's my understanding that in that year, you didn't need a birth certificate to enroll a child in school. I remember reading in the school office, and then I heard I was going to first grade. My school records had an error in my birth year, though.

By the time I finished first grade, I had heard that there was a war. I didn't quite understand much about what they talked of, but I knew my mother said they were fighting somewhere with machine guns, so I was not to worry. I didn't actually know what a machine gun was, but I did know that guns could kill. Little by little, the New York that I recognized seemed to change. The New York that I have become familiar with was filled with the things that I love to do.

On a Saturday, my mother used to take me to 125th St.; we would ride the trolley car to get there. We didn't own a car, which wasn't unusual because many people didn't own cars in New York City. It was fun to ring the bell on the trolley. I also loved to ride the double-decker bus. Some Sundays, when we came from church, my mother would take me on the public double-decker bus, and we would ride all the way downtown.

My mother would pay the fair to go back up to Harlem, and it was a great round-trip ride for 20 cents.

Years later, I did that by myself. There was almost always something fun to see.

Almost all the adults I knew seemed to like baseball, and there was always talk of the Yankee Stadium if you liked the NY Yankees and the Polo Grounds or the New York Giants. My mother was a Brooklyn Dodgers fan, and in that case, you almost always had to love Ebbets Field, where the Dodgers played. My mother took me to a Dodger game with her friend when I was pretty young. I didn't know at all what was going on, but it seemed like fun. The part I liked so much was my mother buying a hot dog for me from one of the vendors who had a pan around his neck with hot dogs!

My father, Nee Edward, nicknamed Baber, was a reality in my world, not because I saw him but because I always heard of him. I'm not even sure of how many times I got to see my father. Before, I remember thinking about him as my father. He had a big black 4-door car. I'm sure he took me for rides in that car. I just don't remember, but I do remember telling the children in the neighborhood or near the house I lived in not to touch my father's car!

My father visited my uncle, and my brain could not tell me anything specifically. **However, a thought just came into my head as I recalled the instances since my mother lived in that house, too; I wondered if my father and my mother talked to each other when he visited New York. (I don't understand what you mean here. You wonder if they talked before they hung out, or after they broke up?)** I wonder, I wonder.

Chapter One

So, readers, tell me or reflect on this: Do you think he and my mom saw each other whenever my dad came to New York? Especially since he was staying downstairs and she was upstairs on the 3rd floor. They must have seen each other in passing. This is a new thought that I have never asked myself before. It is only now, as I sit here and write my story that it jumps out to me and makes me wonder.

I hope that they did, and I hope they were nice to each other. My father took me every day to get my favorite cracker, ginger snaps. Most of the time, I remember we went there every day. But because it's all one big setting for me, I cannot remember anything specific.

My father had left to go back to South Carolina early in the morning, and I remember I was outside playing near where his car had been parked. I do remember a man grabbing me, and I didn't scream right away. I didn't know who the man was, though. I'm not sure why I was confused and didn't, but my play brother JR., who had been near the car, saw him when he grabbed me and he screamed out.

The story that I was told over and over was that the man headed towards the roof with me, and JR ran up the stairs behind the man to the floor where we lived. He screamed for the adults to come and said, "A man had Ida and was going to the roof." I'm told that the man let me go before he got to the roof, and as far as I remember, he was never seen again.

Chapter Two

New York is Changing

New York City was changing in other ways. There was talk about the war in Europe. People were concerned about whether or not the war could come to our country. The United States residents, by and large, did not know what WWII was except through the movies. Radios blasted the news everywhere, reaching inside our apartment, too.

I heard the radio and the newscasters, but at my age, I didn't relate to what they were talking about. And none of the adults that I was around explained any of it to me. It was discussed a little bit in school because we had to learn about air raid shelters and practice for air raids.

Yet, I was just six years old and too young to fully understand what war was all about. I still colored my books and cut out paper dolls. However, my godmother was in charge of the apartment and watching out for all of us.

She did not work, so she was home during the

day, and so she signed up to become an Air Raid warden. She wore the belt, sash, and caps that identified her as an Air Raid warden. She was to monitor our house and the apartment house next door's lights in the evening whenever there was a practice air raid. This was to make sure that we fit the required restrictions of not sending light through our windows.

I do remember a standing lamp that we lit partially at the base. If you turned off the lights on the top of the lamp, the lighting from the base could be kept on and provide sufficient light for you to see without casting a glow on the windows. We were in stealth mode, playing hide-and-seek.

During those weeks, my family spoke of my father being sick, and then a telegram came with the news that my father, Edward Brown, had died! That tall, slim, handsome man who wore the brown cap with the brim on the side of his head, who had held my hand in his big hand when he walked me to the store to get my favorite treat, ginger snaps, had died. I was also told he died in his mother's arms, my grandmother Ida. I'm not sure if I knew then what it all meant.

Sickness and death were new to me. I didn't know how final it was. So, as I write this now, I'm crying! My father, who I hardly knew, was dead, and that meant I would never see him again! Some days later, I had no idea how many people had come to our apartment, and I was in bed at the time. It was their mission to show his 6-year-old daughter two pictures of her father lying in a casket, stiff and with his eyes shut.

Chapter Two

I was so overwhelmed with fear that I didn't want to look at those pictures at all. I didn't want to remember them either…but for years, I could never get the vision out of my mind. It was difficult because I've only had three pictures of my father in my lifetime. Those two pictures I never wanted to remember, nor did I want them near me. The third was of him and I eating ginger snaps, which are still my favorite crackers. I don't eat them much anymore, but they're still my favorite!

And believe me, when I eat them, I think of my dad briefly every time. I was in the 1st or the 2nd grade when my father died. I remember school as a pleasant place to be despite stuff. I liked school, especially when we had cold milk and cookies in the morning, but I was not prepared for the event of December 7th, 1941!

The newspapers everywhere said that Pearl Harbor had been bombed, and I remember my teacher in school explaining to us as best she could what that meant. It frightened me! Everywhere, again, the radios took up the broadcasting time because that's all we heard was the event of the bombing of Pearl Harbor on December 7th, 1941, and the next day on December 8th, 1941. The United States declared war on Japan, and subsequently, Italy and Germany, the Japanese allies, declared war on the United States!

The United States was now in full participation in World War 2. It seemed like one day, everyone had been laughing and having fun, and afterward, when war was declared, there was no more fun. Days later, I learned that my two adult cousins were thinking of enlisting in the military.

One cousin eventually went to the European sector, and the other went to the Asian sector. Several weeks later, my mother got a new job working with the railroads in New York City. She was part of support teams on the railroad, which had something to do with the war effort.

My mother explained that she would have to work nights when she started the job. She was in charge of a team. Things had changed, and my uncle Curtis and his family had moved a few months earlier to 148th St. Though they moved, they had always made it possible for me and my mother to visit them. I could take a short bus trip to visit. I was still living with my godmother, my play sister Arletha, and her mother, who were in our apartment.

Arletha was 12 years old, and I loved her dearly. She took the time to explain to me what she knew about the war by sitting me down and explaining the details about the war. This was based on what was told to them in school.

I was happy I had her around me because my play brother JR had moved away from my area. I missed him, and I didn't have him to watch out for me when I was playing outside. So, I had to stay inside the apartment most of the time. My godmother babysat other kids, and we often played house in the kitchen. We did puzzles, coloring books, paper dolls, and comic books with two cats who were always around.

I remember seeing posters during that time of Uncle Sam with his finger pointed out, with the subtitle,

Chapter Two

"Uncle Sam wants you!" I heard friends of my godmother and others saying their relatives were enlisting in the war, and it sounded pretty scary. I also heard the family and friends speak about food rationing. There would also be shoe rationing.

I knew they also spoke about gas rationing, but that didn't mean very much to my family because we didn't have a car. However, when sugar was to be rationed, that scared me. How would we eat? I didn't understand some of it at all.

I'm not quite sure what came over me in the next few years during the war. I don't know if I was unhappy or happy. As I look back now, it was a state of being. I did things that I shouldn't have. Even though I was protected and cared for, I remember going up to the rooftops and running across from roof to roof. On the streets, you were subject to scary things that the adults spoke of, so instead of playing out on the streets, we played on the roofs.

I doubt if it was with permission. It's important to know that people went on the rooftops for fun. Before I lost my photos, I had numerous pictures of myself in my Sunday's best, taken on a rooftop. It was not unusual for a family to have a party on the rooftop. Houses were joined together sometimes by the roof, but often, there was an opening that if you jumped across and missed it, your life was over.

On one occasion, I foolishly did it. It wasn't a good feeling, and I knew when I did it that I would never do it again. Months later, one of the kids on the block died from such an attempt. But I did other things that were just as foolish. I can tell you that throughout my lifetime until I was about 50 years old, I would have nightmares of falling from a building…

There were few, if any, television sets in New York City during WWII. Few people had telephones, but we had movie theaters. When you go to the movies, it is customary to see "The World News" as it was identified. You saw the bombings and the occurrences of how our U.S. troops were keeping the peace in Europe and Asia as far as the military was concerned. Most of the time, it was quite fearful because there was that concern that our country could be attacked and bombed, too.

As I grew older, I was able to live full-time with my mother in her apartment on 128th St. When she was home with days off, I was with her, and when she couldn't be home, I would go and stay by my godmother. I will confess that I did not always go where I was supposed to.

I was attending an elementary school that was accessible from both addresses, and I can admit that I played hooky from school and from the summer program occasionally. Whenever my mother found out, it was not good for me. Yes, I got punished. I remember being unable to play in the neighborhood, and I would often stay on the fire escape looking at the buildings surrounding where I lived.

So when the war ended, I was ten years old, and my mom took advantage of the offer from my uncle and aunt for me to spend three weeks with them uptown. I was excited. I had visited them on weekends before, but

Chapter Two

I knew nothing really about that part of upper Harlem. My two cousins, who had been in the war, had returned to Harlem to live with their sister, who had a love for photography and a great job there. I was hoping to learn how to take pictures.

They also shared their house with a wonderful dog named Prince. He was a German shepherd. I can remember years ago, when they lived in the same building, they would put me on Prince's back. I was looking forward to spending time with them all. It was always fun in their house, but outside their doors, I wasn't too sure. The first day, when my aunt sent me to the store to buy something for her, there was a problem.

About three kids my age actually tried to jump me and take the money. They did not succeed, but they got in my face and told me how they were going to beat me up because I wasn't from that area. Then they said they had to beat me up so I would know who was in charge. I felt so bad that I had to go and tell my aunt and uncle what had happened. I told her that I didn't want to go out because they wanted to fight me, and I didn't want to fight.

My aunt Genia decided to intervene. She called all the girls together that she could find and brought me into the conversation. She told them that she expected the best from them and that I was her niece. "I want you all to get along and be friends." She encouraged us all in her unique and particular way that day.

It was wonderful! That summer, I made friends who remained friends for many years. I never forgot that day because I was aware of New York City and street violence, but I never experienced anything like that. While I grew up without sisters or brothers, I was always a friendly soul. I was not overly friendly but knew how to mingle safely as I grew older. I joined PAL, and it was common for me to be home in the apartment on 128th Street by myself.

There were two bedrooms, the kitchen in the living room, and the fire escape. I spent a lot of time on the fire escape when the weather was good or warm. I wrote stories, colored, read books, and listened to the radio. Less and less, I would go by my godmother since Aletha was old enough to have a boyfriend, so it wasn't the same. Yet when I could play on the playground on 128th Street, I did. I jumped rope, roller skated, played dodgeball, and hide-and-seek. When I was at my house, I practiced dancing.

This is an interesting part of my lifetime that I do remember visually. I learned how to dance the current dances by dancing with my refrigerator! It was a time when hand dancing was very popular. There were the jitterbugs. There were the Savoy dancers, and we got to see that type of talent as television began to emerge.

My mother was the first person in her apartment building to have a television, and it was so like my mother. I don't know how she got people to pay to come and see television, but she did. She never shared that with me, but many times when The Ed Sullivan Program was on, we'd have six or seven chairs in the hallway and people in the living room sitting around watching TV.

When I was about 11 years old, my mother had

Chapter Two

arranged the schedule for me to leave the house at about noontime. I'm not sure why I wasn't in school, but I understood the arrangement. It was a usual thing, so it didn't come with any stress. I had grown up on 131st St. I didn't have any problems going to that street where I had lived for years. I was beginning to know the kids on 128th St., so when I left the apartment that day, I saw a couple of my new friends.

They had the jump rope out, and I decided to jump rope. Then they asked me if I could stay and play a couple of games afterward, and I agreed. I guess as I was crossing the street, I got hit by a small panel truck. I never knew what hit me because when I woke up, I was in the hospital. My mother had come home from work only to be met at the subway station by concerned neighbors telling her that I was in the hospital.

I was shocked to wake up in the hospital. I had never been in the hospital before that, and I was sad because my mother was so upset with me that I didn't do what she had told me to do. I was in the hospital for three or four days, and then a week later, they sent me to a "convalescent home." I assumed that my mother had been involved in adult arrangements to send me to the "convalescent" home, but I didn't know what it was all about.

I was scared when it was time to go to the home because I thought it meant a concentration camp. WWII had ended, but I had no one to tell me what to expect from this convalescent home. In these homes, I heard stories about lost and molested children. I had been a victim in the sense I had no one to talk to when someone tried to put their hands in my pants or express my issues with life.

When I got there, I sensed it. It was so far away from what I was used to in terms of playing and being around other children and people. So let me explain what I mean: it was far outside of New York City, far upstate NY. I was the only African American child there. Everyone who worked there was white except one of the ladies, who was a kitchen employee. She was an African American person on the property who worked as a cleanup person in the kitchen.

I'm not sure why I was sent there. She saw and smiled at me once or twice but never spoke to me. There were about 37 children there, as best I could recall. I think we had three or two dormitories of about 15 or 16 children in each.

I got there just in time for dinner and was introduced. I had not been prepared to be sent away, and I had not been told much about where I was going. I was cut off from communication with my mother. There were no cell phones. We were told we could only write and receive letters.

My mother had paid a lot of money to get my hair properly done for my management. However, the first thing they did was shampoo my hair and check for lice. Big Problem! What to do with my hair? My hair should not be washed every day! How will it dry? Thankfully, I could braid enough for looks. The afro was not around in 1946! You needed proper hair supplies for that kind of hair management.

So, I sense some smiles on a few reader's faces. Yet it was traumatizing for me. I had never in my life

Chapter Two

been put in that type of situation, so I had no knowledge of how to deal with what had happened to me. I felt so different, so exposed!

The situation didn't get any better because, at their discovery, I could braid. They assigned me four girls, and I was responsible for braiding their hair every morning after it was washed. This was done before we had breakfast and did our activities for the day.

I mentioned that because I have no idea or memory of anything else that we did there. I remember the showers, and I remember the hair washing. I remember that we played games. I remember writing my mother and getting a card from her once. Also, I remember when it was time for me to go home. I was so excited.

They put me on the train, and I understood that my mother would meet me at Grand Central Station. I'm certain that my mother knew more than I knew. I'm sure of that because my mother was waiting at Grand Central station when I arrived. This next part is a joke that my Mom and I laughed about for years.

I was so excited and happy to see my mother that I ran over to her and said, "Mama, Mama." She looked at me like she did not know who I was. She didn't even get up off the bench. And then she said, "Idamay! Is that you? Oh my God…what happened to you? What happened to your hair?"

She told me to sit down on the bench and reached into her hair, where she had a small side comb. She tried to put my hair into a less wild look so we could ride home on the subway. From the subway, she took me to the hairdresser. Yes, that story came up and has been told dozens of times in my life, but never involved how to soothe my humiliation.

I knew I had changed a lot, and maybe I was changing after my experience in the convalescent home. I was becoming a little bit of a loner, and I didn't feel too lonely or uncomfortable with myself. It was not unusual for me as I grew older to get on the bus when my mom was working on the weekend and ride all the way down to NYU and come back home.

In the 6th grade, as I was getting ready to graduate and go to junior high school, I was excited about it. I had finished many projects in my class, and I love doing projects. I was looking forward to getting a couple of awards. We had a major project to do. I did my project a day early, and I completed the essay on time. I don't remember how many pages the essay was, but I remember it was written on the front and back of the loose-leaf paper report.

When I got to class, my teacher called me up to her desk and told me that my essay was unacceptable. It wasn't about the quality; it was because I had written on the back of the paper. She explained you know better. It was said in front of the class, and I was humiliated and embarrassed.

Up to that point, I had always loved Ms. Siegel. She was our choir director, and I loved singing in the choir. I'm not sure what happened to me, but I was so angry. I went and opened my desk because we had desks

Chapter Two

that had compartments. I threw the papers into the desk, and if that wasn't bad enough, since I was visual in front of everyone, I let the desk lid slam down as hard as it could.

The sound reverberated in the room, and everybody looked shocked. The teacher looked at me furiously and saw what I had done. She said to me, "Get out, get out! Go down to Mrs. Kellner's room." She was the 5th-grade teacher who was her friend, " and stay there until your mother comes to school."

In addition, she said, "You're taking no work. I will not give you any work while you're there. You cannot read comic books while you are there. You are to sit there in your punishment until your mother comes."

Well, my mother informed me that she wasn't coming even though I explained to her that I could not be promoted out of the 6th grade until she came. I remember her saying she was tired of me doing things like this because she had to work and could not miss a day's work by coming to school, etcetera, etcetera. I really thought she would come. But I should have known my mother, Maggie Lewis, better than that.

I stayed in that class for two weeks. My mother finally came, and I don't remember if all was forgiven, and I don't remember what consequences other than being put out of the classroom I suffered. I got no awards, obviously, but I did get promoted, and I went to an all-girl junior high school in an Irish and Italian neighborhood on the fringes of Harlem.

The problems surrounding my promotion to 6th grade made me sometimes wonder if my mother loved me. Looking back now, I realize I never tried to understand her. I just couldn't understand why we couldn't talk. Sometimes, I tried to explain my point of view, but to my mom, "Life was hard, and that was why she had to work hard. I needed to understand that. I needed to work hard in school and learn the lessons so I could get a good job and maybe even go to college."

My cousin, my father's niece, was going to graduate soon from high school, and I knew she talked about different jobs after she graduated. I had heard her say she wanted to take French in high school. That, too, was strange to me, but even so, I just listened, and I rarely asked questions.

Many times, when I was on the fire escape, I read and thought about things. I would do silly but often dangerous tricks on the fire escape. We lived on the 3rd floor. Sometimes, I even felt as though my mom would probably be better off if I were dead; then, she wouldn't have to work so hard all the time.

I would dress up, comb and fix my hair, wear a pretty dress, and pretend. One day, from the fire escape, I happened to be looking around at the other apartment buildings, and I saw that a woman had climbed out of her apartment to stand in the window. Unbelievably, she jumped from that sixth-floor apartment building.

I heard when her body hit the ground!! I cannot think that I was the only one who saw her. I never had time to scream. I never had time to think. I stayed in

Chapter Two

shock! As I think about it, and I have thought about it many times. I realize that my foolish child play activities from the fire escape could cost me, even if not death, serious injury. I promised myself never to do such foolish things again. I never did. For at least 40 years of my life, I had nightmare dreams of falling from a building.

1946 was a great new start for me. I had been promoted to the 7th grade, and my new school was a girls junior high school, JHS 159, located on 119th St between 1st & 2d Ave. Looking at the school from a distance and even close up, inside of it, you would scream out, "Oh No! 159 was a school building that was about 75 years old, and it looked it! At the time, I remember thinking it looked so awful, almost like a prison on the outside, yet after weeks of going to the school and having fun with my new classmates, I lost that concern about what the building looked like, inside and outside. Now, I can't remember it at all.

JHS 159 was far from my home and actually on the fringes of Harlem, and even though I enjoyed the school, the walk from home to school was a long one. Eventually, we (my neighborhood friends from Harlem) got transportation passes to go back and forth, but when the weather was nice we walked, we talked, and we laughed and had fun. We got to share our cultures through our walks.

For most of us out of Harlem, it was our first opportunity to mix regularly with others our age and older from a different culture. I ate my first Hero sandwich in the Italian deli right across the street from our school. We got Hero sandwiches for ten and fifteen cents. We learned how to say some Italian phrases, laughed and talked about the words we were learning.

There was a boy's school, near us but several blocks away, named Cooper JHS on the fringes of Harlem. Their building was brand new, and we were told it was our "brother" school. We never went there, but I remember some of their students coming to our School for an event. We were told that our school would be rebuilt into a modern school like Cooper Junior High School.

On our way home, we also passed a jelly Donut bakery. They were the best-ever jelly donuts, and you got 3 for 10 cents. Granulated sugar on the outside with the real jelly inside. Often inside the bakery, they would pile up the jelly donuts up against the window so you could see them, and to be perfectly honest, we would see roaches crawling on the window, but we still bought those donuts!!

The community of Harlem was all black, with very few mixed nationalities. So many of my new friends had great attitudes and good behavior. Their sense of purpose and interest in school and community activities started to rub off on me. My personality was starting to change, but I still had a long way to go for real self-improvement.

Many of my school friends had sisters and brothers and were in big families. Certainly, they had a lot more people in their house than I did, and even though I went to visit some of them, they weren't always able to come and visit me because my dear mother was working. I got a little tired of always going where someone

Chapter Two

else wanted to go. My play brother, JR's mother, and my mother had stayed friends, and we visited each other on occasion. One Sunday after church, my mother told me I could go and spend some time with him and his mom.

I was pretty excited about that because, to me, he was really like a big brother, and to him, I was like his little sister. There was a two-year difference in our age, and quite frankly, he never let me forget that he had saved my life! To get to his house, I had to take two buses, and that wasn't a problem at all for me since I was very capable of getting around New York City by bus and subway on my own.

It was a two-block walk from the bus stop to his apartment house. As I walked to his street, I happened to notice a young man from the bus seemed to be going in the same direction as I was. There wasn't any kind of red flag in my head about him. It just seemed to be interesting that we were going in the same direction.

When I got to the apartment building where I was going to turn, he ran into the house ahead of me. He went through the door before I came in. That kind of surprised me, but I was thinking more about my visit than being concerned about him.

When I got up to the top of the first floor, there were probably about ten stairs I had to climb. I was shocked to see that same young man with a knife (It looked like a switchblade knife) pointed at me. My heart stopped for a moment because I was in shock. I was 12 years old going on 13, and here I was facing a man with his switchblade pointed at me. (I think he probably was about 21 to 25 years old.)

I was so scared!! He said, "You're going with me up to the roof, or I will hurt you!" To this day, I can't explain what gave me the strength and the foresight to say to him what I said, "I can't go with you up to the roof. My brother was looking out the window when I came into the building. If I don't show up right away, he's gonna be looking for me."

At that moment, a door behind the man opened, and he quickly ran downstairs. Whoever opened the door behind him was someone I didn't know who just happened to be in the apartment on the 2nd floor. At that time, I didn't know enough or have the passion enough to thank God for my safety which was before me then. I just took off and started running up two more flights to JR's apartment.

I was so relieved but still overwhelmed with fear and shaking. Two of his friends were there with him. I knew one of them, and the other one was his neighbor, a guy named Bill. They immediately ran down the stairs when I told them what had happened, looking for the man, but he was long gone. I was aware after that incident that there was a segment of the population of men that was not to be trusted.

In some cases, those whom the family trusted couldn't even be trusted. As I stop and think now, I don't remember if I told my mother about this, and I say this because she must have been upset and very concerned. But I'm sure she knew because I told JR and figured he would have told his mother. So I can't remember what

Chapter Two

my mother said, but that was before my 13th birthday. I was tall, so maybe I appeared older.

I realized I had to be very careful as I came and went places. Sometimes, I wondered if some of my trauma was that I had to live on a quiet level because I didn't really have sisters or brothers to share my concerns with. I didn't have anyone that I could sit down and talk to about these things.

Some things you just kept to yourself, I guessed. My play sister Aletha had grown up with many problems of her own. In fact, she had a baby and was to get married. Even though we still loved each other, I didn't feel comfortable telling her about this issue or asking her advice.

I don't know if telling someone about these problems would have alleviated them. I don't know if I felt better not telling my mother things because she would get very upset with me. I kept many things to myself. I can remember a male family member (no names mentioned here) who knew where we lived coming to my house one afternoon and knocking on the door.

When I said, "My mother isn't home," I didn't open the door because I knew better. He said, "Ohh, I'll come in and just wait till she comes home." I never opened the door, and by the same token, I never told my mother until years later about it.

JHS 159 was to prepare for high school in New York City, where you would go to finish the basic education required for a high school diploma. I volunteered for lots of things in school. I had not chosen a high school I wanted to attend, but my very good friends who lived in my area and some of my newer friends had all planned to go to Julia Richman High School.

One of my best friend's sisters was in the 10th grade at Julia Richman, so that's what I wanted. My guidance counselor told me it would be hard for me to get into Julia Richman HS because they had high academic standards. They also had high personal values for their students.

Yet, my guidance counselor didn't discourage me. She told me to just do as much as I could to be the best person I could be, and we'd see what happened. I changed my attitude and my personality to the highest level at JHS 159.

I read the Bible in the assemblies. I made sure I was one of the best Bible readers ever, a tutor, and a handy person for the teacher. I recited poetry in our assemblies. I made myself eligible for Julia Richman High School by valuing myself.

I never shared what I was doing with any of the adults in my life. I was pretty quiet about it. My friends knew that I was set on going to Julia Richman HS. Not one adult worked with me or knew what I was doing. In my mind and my spirit, I could hear my mother's voice within me.

"Learn, go to school, and get a good job!" she did not have that opportunity. Yet she always encouraged me." My grandmothers, Ida and Charlotte, were there in

Chapter Two

spirit telling me the same thing, saying you can do it!

Chapter Three

Growing Pains

In January of 1949, I got accepted into Julia Richman High School and was so excited. At graduation time from Junior High School 159, I got several awards. My mom was proud of me. She didn't know what I had gone through. She actually never knew too much about some of the things that I was going through in the 7th and part of 8th grade until many, many years later when I shared stories with her.

When I got into Julia Richman High School, I was very proud. I was so thrilled that I had been assigned a mentor and "Aunt Julia," who was a high school senior. I made up my mind then that I wanted to be an Aunt Julia (a type of peer mentor) when I got to the 12th grade.

During my first and second year at Julia Richman HS, it was great. I had many of my same friends from JHS 159. Julia Richman was mid Manhattan on the east side of New York. I took the Lexington Avenue subway to school every day.

There was a group of four, five, or six of us that traveled home with each other every day. We had lots of laughter, serious study, serious issues, and serious teachers in a school of 4,000 girls, all with different lifestyles. The students came from a multiplicity of backgrounds: Italian, Irish, German, Irish, Chinese, Puerto Rican, Jamaican, Greek, Turkish, Southern, and many more, including those from Harlem backgrounds, which was somewhat diverse. Their course offerings were: Academic, Commercial, General, and CO-OP.

As usual, most of the students and many of my friends came from families where they have sisters and brothers, often aunts and uncles, living with them and being around them. I had a couple of cousins on my mother's side who were now living in New York City, and my mom opened her doors to them. I saw them regularly, and in some cases, when needed, I even babysat. My aunt and Uncle Curtis, as well as my cousins, never stopped being there for family comfort and support. Yet I kept my thoughts about my life pretty much to myself and my close friends.

One day, when I came home from school, I was surprised to see my mom at home and sitting in the living room talking to her friend. A man who had come to the house a couple of times was
sitting in the living room.

My mom took me into the kitchen and shared some bombshell news with me! She blew me away because She had gotten Married! I was stunned! I didn't see that coming at all! He had dinner once at our house and told me she knew him before I was born. I couldn't

Chapter Three

believe it!

He was going to move in! She explained to me in a short conversation that she needed the financial help. I was pretty devastated! I told her I had to go to the library, and I left the house and went around the corner to my best friend Corinne's house and cried!

Trouble was on the horizon within a few weeks. I'm not sure how well the new husband thought he knew my mother. Unfortunately, he made a big mistake in his judgment because he wanted my mother to put the apartment under his name.

That wasn't gonna happen at all! He went from being tolerable as the new stepfather to being intolerable as husband and stepfather. He had a city job, and I'm assuming he had a stable income. My mother was still working every day, and I could not find anything that we had in our house that we didn't have before. Yet my mother didn't really discuss bills with me throughout my life. She worked hard. We had things we wanted and ate all the time from a fairly good menu.

We had a TV when no one else in our building had one. We had a refrigerator in a house when others still had ice boxes. I can't remember discussing money with my mother in a way that would have let me know that she was behind in her bills or ahead in her bills. Like many other people in our area, my mother played the "numbers."

There were times when she won money and many more times when she lost. So, I don't recall ever truly learning from my mother why she decided she had to get married. Love? I doubt it; I had never seen any evidence of love between the two of them. Yes, it's friendship because I saw them laughing and talking together in the beginning.

As the days, the weeks, and then months passed by, there seemed to be a lot of tension in the house between my mother and her new husband. Often, my mother would invite family and friends to the house. If I'm not mistaken, we went to a couple of family events as a family and with her new husband, who was originally from Barbuda or Antigua. My mother had a passion for the islands, and many of her friends were from Jamaica, Barbados, and now seemingly Antigua and Barbuda.

She loved Caribbean food, and it was always welcomed in the house, whether she prepared it or, in one or two cases, I know her new husband prepared it. The problem began when he started drinking a lot more than he should. Then, the subject of putting the apartment in his name would come up. He would start a barrage of cussing bad words and drinking liquor out of the bottle. He sang songs loudly, played music loudly, and made it difficult for us to go to sleep. My mother often had to get up and go to work with little sleep.

It was the same for me. So one Friday, when I came home from school with my best friend, Corrine, who lived around the corner, he was at home. He did everything he could to be as obnoxious as he could!

He had a six-pack of beer he was drinking. He walked around in his underwear. He turned the radio up

Chapter Three

as loud as he could. When I told him about it, he cussed me and Corinne out, calling us names.

Since we had a telephone, I was able to call my cousins, who were police officers. I explained to them what was going on, and they told me they'd be there in an hour. They actually arrived in thirty minutes, fully dressed in uniform. Of course, he was somewhat ludicrous because all he kept saying to them was, "Show me your badge, show me your badge."

They explained to him that they expected a different type of behavior as an adult male toward me and if he continued his behavior, especially with my best friend Corrine there as a witness to say it had happened, they would lock him up. He didn't say too much to them other than "Show me your badge." When they left, he went into his bedroom, got dressed, took his beer, muttering and cussing under his breath, and left. He came back the next day. I told my mother what had happened when she came home.

She was pretty angry, and she went into the bedroom, got a big bag and his old suitcase and put his clothes and stuff in it. The next day, Saturday, my mother went to the hardware store, where they changed the locks and got the locksmith to come to the apartment and change the lock on the door. We got a new set of keys and waited for the soon-to-be ex-husband.to arrive so she could give him his clothes and send him on his way.

I stayed close to home with my mother all of Saturday because we didn't know what was going to happen. My cousins called to make sure we were all right, and I explained to them that he had left, but we expected that he would return. He did return at about 4:30 p.m. that Saturday afternoon.

He put his key in the door, and it didn't work. We heard him banging on the door. My mother heard him banging on the door, and she got his clothes and old suitcase. She opened the door, gave it to him, and said goodbye. He literally stayed outside the apartment door cussing bad words until the neighbor came outside with his German Shepherd dog, and he left with his stuff.

Sometimes, he was quiet, but he often behaved outrageously after a few beers. He got the point, and within six months, my Mom had gotten a divorce. His behavior had become a standard joke in and around a few friends and even on my mother's side of the family. Some of the things he did my mom tried to hide from people. He had been quite disruptive, but my mother and I prayed together after he left that he was out of our lives for good.

Even so, we were a little concerned about how the apartment house was built. There was a long corridor and an apartment at the end of the hallway. However, there was a stairway to the left of the corridor and a door to the basement.

Behind the stairwell, and slightly adjacent, was a radiator that allowed a few people to stand before going up the staircase or entering the rear apartment. Our apartment building was one of two twin 6th-floor apartment houses, and we lived on the 3rd-floor rear. There was a total of 18 apartments in each building.

Chapter Three

I was concerned that maybe he would sneak back into the house and bother me, but I had gotten an after-school job and was excited about that. I told my mother that we would make it.

My mom said, "Yes, we would." She became very protective of me and emphasized how important it was for me to finish school. She wanted me to get a good education. The short time period with her husband in the house had caused me to develop a very serious condition of neurodermatitis.

Two years before, during the summer, I spent several weeks with my mother's sister and her husband, my Aunt Bea and Uncle Jesse, and some of my cousins who were still at home. My Aunt Bea had 12 children. The first year, I visited my uncle and aunt, who lived in Lamar, SC. It was really far in the backwoods.

At their home, there were still two of her girls at home who were very close to my age, and my mother had let me visit them two summers back to back. The first time, I rode the train solo from Penn Station to Florence, South Carolina. I was young, not a teenager, but capable, and the ride from Penn Station to Florence took about 15 hours.

I spent most of my days working on the farm in tobacco, climbing in the tobacco barn, helping unload cured tobacco using an outhouse, driving a mule, making butter, milking a cow, chasing chickens, feeding hogs, and eating fresh watermelon. Going to outdoor movies to see Western movies I had seen years prior was also a source of entertainment. It was work, but I learned many things, and I was with family.

When I saw the cotton growing, I knew it was time for me to head home because "putting in tobacco" had been weeks of learning and even fun. If you call working for 20 and 25 cents an hour at the tobacco barn or the field "fun. The boys had fun by throwing big, fat, hefty green tobacco worms on me. I trembled each time one got on me, and after a week or two, I overcame my grossest fears and was able to throw them back at whoever threw them at me.

So nope, I wasn't going to try to pick cotton, not after what I had heard. I was invited to come back to visit my aunt and uncle the next year. They had moved to Hartsville, South Carolina, and that was a good thing. I truly enjoyed being around my cousins Margaret and Olivia, who were close in age to me (one year and three years older). I had another male cousin who was a year older than me, and we got along so well also.

We did so many things that I remember fondly. The weekly Southern Baptist Church experience was wonderful. Meeting other family members who were my older cousins, male and female in church was always cool. They could cook everything you loved to eat just like you wanted it. I met cousins who knew my mother as a child, so I loved many aspects of the visit, hearing things about my mother that she never told me. Eventually, a few of my cousins,, who were near my age, moved up north. They began to visit our house a lot. I was no longer "alone".

In New York often when I went to church, it was

Chapter Three

usually with an adult. I knew some of the children when I started attending. As I grew older and lived with my mother, I didn't know the children in the church because I didn't live in the same area that they did. New York City and Harlem was filled with so many churches I'd often come in and just sit in the pews if I were by myself.

So when my Mom told me after our bad experience with her new husband that we were going to take about eight days and go down to South Carolina to spend time with her sister and her husband, instead of me going to visit by myself, I was happy. We could only stay a week, but it would be great. The doctor had told me if I calmed my nerves, my skin would stop breaking out, so this trip would help.

Everything I loved to eat and more was going to be available. My cousins and I would always have something to laugh and whisper about. I loved that there were always new cousins to meet and games to play. My experiences when I visited South Carolina, including my mother's visit and other large gatherings with my cousins, were sometimes difficult and not all fun and games. There were misunderstandings, and depending on who it was with, it either lasted 5 minutes or 5 days. Of course, I was also the youngest of first cousins, and many of the adults were much older.

I thought about the fact that I was close from where my father's side of the family had lived and created a lifestyle for themselves. I went to Florence several times with my uncle, aunt, and cousins. The train from New York's Penn Station stopped in Florence, and that's where my family picked me up from. I had no connection at that time and no knowledge that anything about my father could be available to me.

Yet, I came to know my family in a different way than in my lifestyle in New York City. One or two became my confidants. There was jealousy, bonding, and shared experiences that many of us talked about and shared for years. Several bonded with me for a lifetime and are still loosely connected to me. Many still remember me now, knowing that I'm the last of my generation.

I have to acknowledge my family from South Carolina and pay tribute to them because our origins of life and greatness began there. I want to pay homage to my grandmother Charlotte on my mother's side, as well as all the family leaders. My mother learned to work hard and consistently on her mother Charlotte's farm. She always spoke about how hard she had worked from my early years.

Tributes to my father, Edward's side, my grandmother, Ida (my namesake), and my grandfather Patrick. Florence County, South Carolina, and its outskirts for both families were rich in my roots. When I was a child, my mom shared with me that she met my father, Edward, in March 1934 because he drove the hearse for the Undertaker who buried her mom, Grandma Charlotte's funeral, in South Carolina.

I never asked my Mom if the families knew each other; however, about 20 years ago, one of my cousins, my mother's niece who lived most of her life in Florence, told me she knew who my grandmother was.

Chapter Three

She described her and her house to me, saying that she was a very nice older lady. I'm now a bit overwhelmed, and I realize it is important to pay tribute to all of them from that area and that time. On both sides, their legacy, dreams, and struggles are perhaps known and unknown by the new generations, forgotten or not recognized, and many untold stories are held. Yet the lineage continues through me and this book!

My mother and I enjoyed our trip together, and it helped clear up old wounds for her. There was a lot of laughter and tears. Doors were opened for more planned visits. We had a great time and returned just in time for me to prepare for my last "semester" at Julia Richman High School. In 1952, we didn't have semesters in New York, but we had graduations twice a year, usually in January and June. I guess it made education a bit more flexible in meeting student requirements.

The apartment building that my mom and I lived in was changing in upkeep. My mother had lived there for almost 10 years. Things in New York were changing. As I grew older and more aware, I felt challenged because I could now feel or sense that I was not as safe as I thought I was. I was concerned.

My best girlfriends lived near me. We grew up like most teenage girls at our school attending Julia Richman. I had friends in school who were already sexually active. I had second-hand knowledge of teachers and students sleeping together. I lived vicariously and learned what not to do.

My two other friends, the 3 Musketeers, and I did

not have boyfriends. We didn't hang out in our neighborhood. I had long since stopped jumping rope on the sidewalks or roller skating. I didn't go to PAL anymore. Yet I was the same girl who had grown up on 131st Street and 128th Street. My friends and I went to the movies, and we ate downtown on Automat Street.

We went roller skating at the rink. I had to go to the museums for my school reports and many situations. So, my life was well structured even though I was that same girl. I was recognized by many of the older kids. In most cases, we were still distant friends.

Gangs were becoming more visual in their activities at that time. I had seen zip guns carried on the streets, and I knew they fought on rooftops. Although the areas between 128th Street and 131st Street had gangs, I personally had only seen two street fights.

Yet things were changing. The two gangs, the Capitals and The Bachelors, were sometimes on a warpath. To be honest, I don't know what their system was like or what it was about. I was considered a 'good girl.' I wasn't running around; I wasn't hanging out. When I went out, it was with family or friends. I guess that sent a message.

The winter of 1950 brought about changes in my building, and on afternoons when I came home from school, often it was just getting dark. In the corridor where, the radiator would keep the hallway warm, and normally, I would feel a sense of comfort. One evening, there by the radiator, I saw three or four teen males. They did not live in the building.

Chapter Three

I lived on the third floor in the back of the apartment building. Of the three guys, one face was familiar but not as a friend. In those days, New York City was a neighborhood where you kind of knew each other. I suspected these guys were part of a gang.

At this time, these two games were hitting back and shooting back at each other. I can't remember which group was from by which street, but apparently, there was some friction between the 128th St. group and the 131st St. group. Both sides knew me because I grew up in both places. You needed a key to get into the corridor in the past, but things had changed. One of my childhood friends lived in the bottom or rear apartment; he was my buddy. However, he was pretty much scared of his own shadow. I could never depend on him if I needed help.

Soon, it became a regular thing when I came in that they were there if it was cold. Often, I would wait on the steps outside until people came home from work to enter. However, sometimes I would just have to get home. Most times, they would nod at me as I came in and went up the stairs. Truthfully, I expected them to run up the stairs after me, but I would nod back at them and hold my breath. I was scared.

However, one afternoon, when I came in, there was only one of the guys there by the radiator. He spoke out loud to me and stopped me from going up the stairs to my floor. I was so terrified! I was waiting for the knife!

He looked at me clearly, and he was even nice-looking. Maybe 19 years old, but I knew or sensed he was a gang member. He looked me clearly in the face and said–without hesitating, "I want you to be my girl!" (That really sounds weird as I think about it but that's what he said. He didn't say I want you to be my woman. He said I want you to be my girl!) I'm just telling you now. I will be back here in a few days.

I think I stopped breathing! I didn't know what to think or say. We were both looking clearly at each other. Years ago, my Uncle Curtis taught me to look at a person when they were talking to you in the eye. So I was looking at him very clearly. What was I to do? I felt like I was going to die.

I had no illusions; I wanted nothing to do with him. I knew what the girls associated with the gangs had to do and who they had to be being part of the gang. I wanted nothing like that in my life, yet I certainly didn't know what to do. At this point, I didn't know where to go. I didn't know who to turn to. I wasn't going to tell my mother.

I have gone to church since I was about five years old, so I had a sense of value. I knew about praying, but I'm not sure if I ever really prayed about something to change my life. I remember that I was so scared on this day that I started praying.

Even though I didn't tell my mother, I told my best friend, Corinne. (As a reader, what would you have done in this situation if you were me? I sure could have used your feedback back then, too!)

Neither Corinne nor I could come up with a plan that would protect me. I was worried every day; my skin

Chapter Three

broke out again. My hands were a mess. I was scared that even my mother would notice. Three days later, as I came home from school and went down the hallway.

The guy was standing alone by the radiator. He called me and said, "What's your name? I told him, and as I was turning away, he came face to face with me, took my hand, and said, "Don't worry, I'm not going to bother you. You're a good girl. I'm uh leave you alone."

Believe me, I have kept that visual in my head for more than seventy years! No matter how many times I think of this and review it all, I'm always grateful to think of how my Lord saved me. He saved me from the experience of having to deal with this guy, the gang life, and my mother. There would be no way my mother would let me live or exist in such a situation.

Could it have cost her her life? Or cost me my Life?? She would have probably sent me to South Carolina. Then, who knows what could of happened to her?

It was then I started thinking about my future. Did I really want to stay in NY and go to college? Would life be like this for me always? I knew I had to do something, but what? I couldn't seem to break the shackles that were binding me. There was always something going on to confront me that I had no control over, or at least it seemed that way.

In August of 1951, my play brother, JR's neighbor, Willis, whom I knew as Bill, came over to my house to fix the record player. Those were the days of the '78s when our record player broke, and Bill came to our rescue. I had met him the year before he ran after the guy who had tried to kidnap me when going to JR's house. He was JR's friend and neighbor.

Bill had graduated from Samuel Gompers Vocational School the year before. He was great at fixing things. About a month after he fixed the record player, he came to my house and asked if I wanted to play some handball and go get some ice cream.

He liked handball, and eventually, I learned to like it, but I settled for ice cream. He asked my mother if he could take me to the movies. She said "yes," but she made it very clear that we had to be back by 9:30, and absolutely 10pm was the latest. Sometimes, he would even pick me up from my part-time job at NY Hospital near Julia Richman.

Our friendship was blooming, and honestly, I was happy. I had stopped breaking out. Then, Bill decided to take a job in upstate New York. I was kind of sad about that because it meant days and sometimes a week of separation. I was to graduate from Julia Richman in late January 1952.

I had not applied to a college because it seemed so expensive. Yet I was 16, even though my school records stated 17, and I felt I had time before I thought about college and money. My school guidance counselor wanted me to make decisions before Thanksgiving.

She told me that I would receive an academic diploma that would prepare me for college, and she explained that I could get some financial aid. She also

Chapter Three

mentioned Community College of New York (CCNY), which she said would be very low-cost. She explained I would be eligible for a scholarship again if I attended. My friends were knocking on CCNY, so I didn't put forth any real effort to get a scholarship there.

I had always wanted to go to college. My best friend at the time had taken the business program and already had a job that would continue once she graduated. My mother kept telling me how proud she was, which made me so happy. I had accomplished the opportunity that I wanted to become an Aunt Julia (more or less a Mentor) for Freshman students.

I did community work with other students, and overall, I was so glad I had gone to Julia Richman High School. Our school motto was "Knowledge Is Power." As the potential for graduation grew, I was like a "cat on a hot tin roof," and I was so anxious for graduation for the future. Little did I know what the immediate future held in store for me.

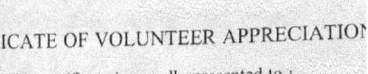

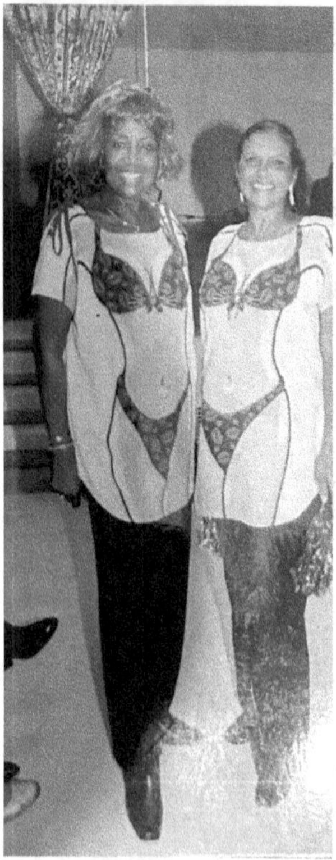

Senator
Lorraine L. Berry

Mother Of The Year Award

Presented To

Dr. Ida M. White

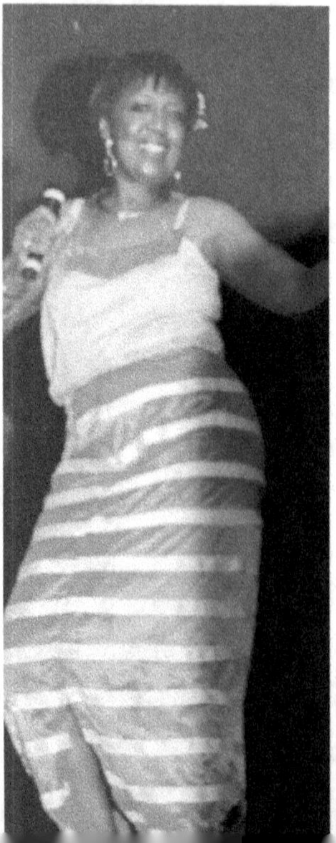

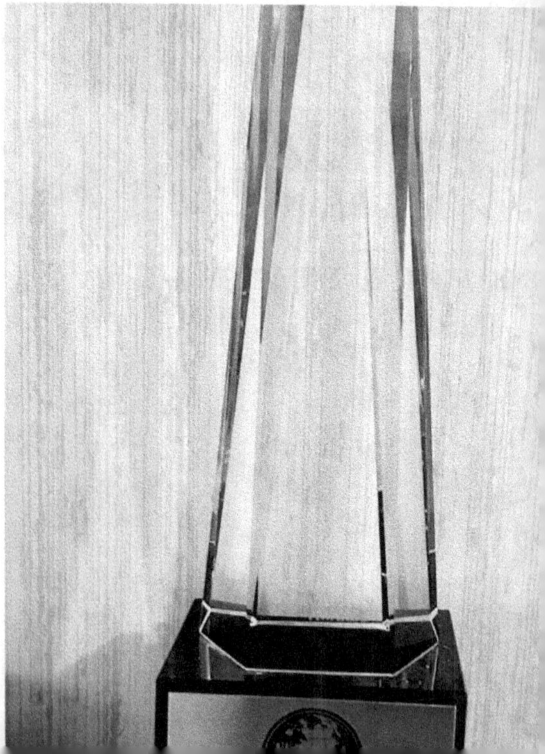

Chapter Four

Julia Richman High School

All of my close friends, who were students at Julia Richman High School, were excited to be going back to school the week after Labor Day. This would be my last year of high school, and it began on September 10, 1951. I was excited about going back to school, and Bill was happy for me since I was going to be graduating soon. Since the summer, we have become close friends. He was a great listener, and I found that he could help me with algebra and mathematical concepts.

My mother had been very specific about my comings and going with Bill. She had told both of us that it was important, very important, that I understood her rules. My mother said that I'd have to be in the house by 10 PM and ready to begin my task for the weekend, or whatever the situation might be.

I was quite surprised that she did not come down harder about Bill, but I guess she didn't because she liked him and trusted him. He was good at helping her do things that were a little bit difficult for her to do. He helped her move around heavy items or brought up bags from her shopping trip. He also knew how to fix so many things.

When Bill began his job in Spring Valley, New York, at the Rockland State Mental Hospital in Upstate New York, he was scheduled to begin work at the same time I was going back to school. I was sad because I knew I was going to miss him. Bill explained to me that he would come down to visit on some weekends. So, I was really excited when he told me that he would be coming to visit on Sunday, September 30th.

When the September 30th weekend rolled around, I couldn't wait to see him. He drove directly to my house first and told me that he wanted us to stop by and say hi to his mom, dad, sisters, and brothers. We spent about an hour and a half at their house. After the visit with them, I begged Bill to take me to Coney Island.

It was a special time, and fun just driving to Coney Island laughing and talking. It was a very special time for us together. We hung out there were there from 6:30, walking around Eating hot dogs, doing some rides before we headed back on the road to go to my house by 8:30 PM.

Then, we had a mishap! "A slight problem with the car," Bill said. Bill's car was a 1940's Buick. Bill told me not to worry he knew how to take care of the situation, and he did. He got back on the road to get to

Chapter Four

my house around 9:30 PM. I knew it was going to take us about 45 minutes to get home and the mishap set us back by at least thirty to forty minutes.

I was really scared. Bill tried to reassure me that he would make it in time. Unfortunately, we did not get to my house until 10:20 PM. I'm not sure why I was super scared, but I knew that my mother meant what she said, and I didn't know what she would do or say.

So when we got to my house, I refused to get out of the car. I told Bill to go upstairs to the apartment and tell my mother what had happened. He didn't want to do that, so I stayed in the car and I cried. Then I had an idea! Deep down inside, I was so tired of things not ever working out the right way. I didn't want to come up against another issue of my mother being upset with me so close to my high school graduation.

So I said, "Bill, you know what?" He said, "What?" I said to him, "Let's get married! Let's go to Spring Valley now and get married tomorrow that way being married will protect me from my mother and everyone else. You have a job we can buy a house and and move away."

Bill looked at me seriously, and he said, "You're serious, aren't you?"

I replied, "Yeah!"

He said, "OK, let's go!" and so we took off. By the time we arrived in Spring Valley, New York, at his sister's house, it was almost 2:00 am in the morning.

That whole episode turned out to be a time of confusion. His sister was married to an older man. They shared a two-bedroom cabin with my play brother JR and his wife! All of the conversations centered around how crazy what we were planning was. First of all, they were quite upset that he was coming in so late at night in the early morning, waking them up to ask if I could sleep on their couch.

Eventually, the chaos subsided, and I lay down, but I never slept. Bill slept in his car and went to his job at 6:00 AM. He had promised me that he would return at noon.

By 8:00 AM, I was in the cabin alone with JR's wife, who was pregnant. The others had gone to work. I was frightened and sad about my mother. Yet, I thought she'd be happy that I got married, and she wouldn't have to worry about me anymore.

Bill came to me at 12 noon and was the bearer of bad news! In the Spring Valley, NY, community where we were and the nearby towns, it was a Jewish holiday week, Rosh Hashanah, strictly observed, and as a result, we could not get a marriage license before the next week. I was 16 years old, so of course, I needed my mother's permission.

Bill was over 18 and basically could be arrested for kidnapping me. It was a real pile of bad news. I was stunned! I don't recall much about anything after hearing that. My stomach was churning inside, and when evening came, there was another surprise to greet us.

Chapter Four

My mother sent the local police to the home where we were! I was surprised that my mother had even suspected that I would be there. Yes, I had never even thought she would go searching for me.

The two police officers said that mother, Ms Lewis only wanted to know if Idamay Lewis was there. I am tearing up inside now as I remember the drama. I knew now what a mess I had gotten myself into. I began to realize if I had just gone home and apologized to my mother, and begged her to understand she would have. The drama now was frightening!

The fear that I felt was real! I didn't know what to do especially since marriage seemed to be out of the question. Then Bill delivered another hard blow to me! He told me that under the circumstances I was going to have to return home the next day. He explained to me that I could take the Greyhound bus into New York City to go home.

He said not to worry about it and also let her know he would be there the next day to talk to her. I agreed to it because I had no plans at all. My play brother, JR took me the next day to get the bus, he was very worried because he knew how my mother was. He gave me a big hug, and said to me, "Don't worry everything's going to be all right'.

Everyone makes mistakes in life... Sometimes, they make bad choices. It doesn't make them bad people; it just means they are human. So, I challenge you as the reader to reflect on these two questions:

- What are the steps one can take to make better choices without being too hard on one's self?
- How would you respond if a friend made this same type of mistake?

It was about 3 o'clock when I opened the door to our apartment. My mom was not home, and nothing seemed out of place. I went to my bed and laid down to go to sleep. But I couldn't sleep, and eventually, I heard the key in the door. The apartment was set up with a guard lock pole in the floor, and it was a protection against anyone forcing their way into the apartment.

As soon I heard my mother at the door, I jumped up and went to open the front door. As I stood in front of the door, waiting for my mother to enter, I felt the pains of fear creeping all over me. When my mother entered, she looked at me very coldly and said, "Get out ... Go back to where you have been for the past two days!"

I reached out to her crying and begging her not to put me out. Crying, I said how sorry I was and, she said, "I said get out!" We were still by the door, when, the doorbell rang, and I was surprised. I knew it was not Bill, he was not coming until tomorrow. To my surprise it was my good friend Corrine who lived around the corner.

Apparently, she had come to find out what my mother had learned about my disappearance. She was there to hear my mother say again to me to go back to where I was the last few days. Corinne begged her to forgive me, and God blessed me that she did!

I hugged my mother so much, but she kept push-

Chapter Four

ing me away. She told me that she was so hurt and scared when she didn't hear from me. I told my mother and Corinne that Bill said he would come the next day… Thanks to Corrine, there was some peace, and she and I agreed to talk more at school the next day.

Before my mother went to sleep, she informed me I was to make my own breakfast, and she would not sign a note for me to get back into school. Wednesday, when I got home from school, ohh how I wanted Bill to be there. I was even a little worried in my heart. Corrine and my friends had negative and positive opinions of my choices. I was 16 years old, exhausted and not as hopeful about the outcomes because everything was now so uncertain.

I still wanted the freedom of being married with a car and a house in the suburbs. I also wanted the white picket fence and a dog. So my prayer was for Bill to come and save me. Save me and give me all of the above!!

Bill came about 7:45 PM. That was a big relief! My mother was even friendly. We were happy to put the episode behind us. Yet, weeks later my mother let me know that she realized I was pregnant. I breathed a sigh of relief that she did not go ballistic on me but I was still scared.

She kept so much to herself, and I kept things to myself. She told me plainly that I had better get married. My mother let both of us know that she would not be a part of our wedding or help with the details. Those details would be up to us.

Bill and I decided to get married right after my graduation, which was on January 26, 1952. Graduation was fun and a relief but fairly uneventful. I said goodbye to Julia Richman High School, where I had spent happy days. I said goodbye to friends that I had known since Junior High, realizing that I would probably never see them again. We hugged, kissed, and took pictures on the steps and in front of Julia Richman High School.

They shouted out to me and laughed, "First comes love, then comes marriage, here comes Ida pushing a baby carriage!" It was kind of funny, sort of in a way. My mother was disappointed that I chose not to go to college, but she never brought it up to me for discussion. Perhaps secretly, she was happy about becoming a grandmother. Looking back now, reflecting, I really don't know.

My mother and Bill were able to have a talking relationship. The two of them decided that all of us wanted a house in Nassau County in the suburbs. As a result, we would remain in New York City until we could buy a house. For a time, Bill would move into her apartment on 128 Street. They came to terms on the rent he would pay once we were married.

Bill and I did what was necessary to get married in New York City. I remember we faked signatures on the documents because my mother had told me she would not sign any paperwork. I had written so many documents for my mother in my short lifetime and signed so many notes for her, either with her knowledge or without her knowledge, that I knew how to imitate her signature.

Chapter Four

So, on Saturday, February 2nd, we had a "marriage" but not a wedding! We got married at about 5:30 pm in a church without any fanfare. It was just the two of us, the pastor and his wife.

Bill and I laughed about everything we saw as we drove. We went for a ride across the George Washington Bridge. I don't know why Bill had his trumpet in the car, but we went by the Hudson River near the bridge, and he played the trumpet for me. We were happy.

Bill had promised to teach me how to drive. He would refer to the car as my car. I was so happy when I got my Learner's Permit. Well I didn't have to get up to go to school anymore, but my mother had a list of chores and things I needed to do for myself, my husband, as well as preparation for becoming a mom.

Thus, by early February, when my friends and classmates went off to college, traveling, or going to fun events, at 16 going on 17, I was in a marriage, listening daily to my mother suggesting what we should do and listening to Bill on what we would do and could do. I was struggling to hold on to my dreams because what is life if you don't have a dream?

As I sat one day thinking about what it was like not to be going to school anymore, I felt a little unnerved. The Julia Richman HS Academic Program was so great for me. It provided such high standards for one's accomplishments.

I remember being so happy to get the Aunt Julia award at graduation time for having faithfully served as an Aunt Julia. I missed out on some of the academic awards, but I graduated at 16 with a 2.9 GPA. My algebra kept me from my 3.0 score.

I wanted to go to work and get a job when I finished high school. I remember that when I was in school, we often had work recruiters come from Wall Street. Their purpose was to announce positions coming available. I went to two employment offices and was very proud to fill out the applications and write down that I was a Julia Richman HS graduate because of our success rate in the marketplace.

I was shocked when I was rejected at so many employment offices or personnel offices that I went to looking for employment in New York City!! I had graduated with an academic diploma meaning that I had taken college preparatory courses. I had taken a few minor typing classes also.

So in reality, the racism of the 1950s in New York City had very little available for academic diploma graduates who had no other skills. I had taken typing as an elective course, and my skills were limited but good enough to qualify for many jobs. But I couldn't get a receptionist job in Manhattan because I was "Colored."

In New York City, I was told frankly that I could get a job in the factory, but not in an office. So, I was so excited when friends of mine told me that I could apply for a telephone operators position at the New York telephone company. I knew that operators had to work around the clock, and I didn't think that would work for me. Then I learned that they had a business representative

Chapter Four

position that was in the office.

It was their top position for females, and it didn't require any special skills. The person who told me felt that since I was a graduate of Julia Richman, I could probably get hired because of the quality of my education. I was so happy about that because I was feeling so discouraged. When I went to the New York telephone company, there were hundreds of young ladies waiting to be interviewed, and I was told to come back tomorrow or on another date; I felt hopeless. The personnel office was in Brooklyn, which was not an easy commute for me.

I had grown very tired of the job-hunting rigmarole, and being pregnant was a bit stressful in the early months. However, Bill told me not to think of working until the baby came. Getting ready for the baby was the priority. We were saving money, but we were spending it. He had bought a new car, or a new, used car, a 49 Buick Roadmaster.

It was a perfect car to drive to Nassau County every day with five Riders. They paid him for their ride by the week. It always seem like he was buying tools, etc. While, I was expecting, the money to pile up in our bank account, it wasn't happening. I reminded Bill that we had to begin saving with my mother for the house in Nassau County.

When my baby was born, I continued to stay home as a housewife and a mother to take care of the baby. It all seemed very strange to me because it was a different world than I knew how to process. I felt like I was going crazy sometimes, and when an opportunity came along for a job with Chocks Full of Nuts part-time. I was able to work a job near my home. It was three blocks away from where I lived, and I thought, "How great this is; it will work out fine!"

In the early days of my training, the best thing I could think of about working at Chock Full of Nuts was seeing Jackie Robinson. I got to serve him their Orange Ade once. He had retired from the Brooklyn Dodgers and went to work for the Chock Full of Nuts company as one of their Vice Presidents. I was in training when he came in to visit.

I was beginning to see that the Latin I took in Julia Richman and the Social Studies classes weren't going to help me. I didn't even have to think. It was a ritual type of employment. "Just do what you are told," and your opinion was not asked for or appreciated.

Bill and I had friends and family who were having children. Bill's father had a new addition and was already talking about having both babies christened at the same time in his church. Bill was excited about the idea of working and living in the suburbs of Nassau County. He kept saying I know we'll find our house out there. I always answered, "And a dog too!"

Chapter Five

After Julia Richman High School

I felt that Bill White, who I married, was a catch. He was a good-looking guy. He was a little under 6 ft. Sometimes, when I wore inch heels, we were a little unbalanced as we walked together. So I stuck with 2-inch heels. It was back in the day when short and tall ladies dressed up in heels. He had told me I had beautiful legs. Bill was two years older than me and the oldest son of ten children. He was so talented with technology as it was emerging in the 1950s. He grew up in his role as the oldest son with very strong family ties. His brother, eleven months younger than him, was his best friend.

His dad worked in the US Post Office in New York and had a private side business in hardwood floor maintenance. His mom was a stay-at-home wife and mother. Her tenth child, a daughter, was born exactly two weeks prior to my son, Lester. Bill loved jazz music and the popular rhythm and Blues. Bill was a great trumpet player and good on the saxophone.

He loved having the best-sounding stereo in our home and wherever we were. He always had great high-five music sound and speakers, which was why many people liked to come to our house. Bill could dance but was happier behind the scenes playing the music as a DJ. As the television industry emerged, he was a master TV technician. He was a Jack of all trades, and he mastered all of them as well.

He was always busy. We were on the road driving a lot, sometimes to Virginia and other times to upstate New York. He was not a sports fan, but he loved bowling. He was great at bowling and very competitive. I loved to bowl, too, so we had something in common. For several years, he worked as an apprentice tool and die maker. At one point, we did go into a business together. When it ended, I realized I did much better working at a regular job than working hands-on. I could almost say, looking back, that we were opposites.

Five years after our marriage in 1957, we were able to get the house we fell in love with. I got my dog and realized one dog was enough because I had a new baby, my daughter, Denise. We lived in a neighborhood ideal for raising children in the suburbs of Nassau County.

I went to work at Doubleday Book Company and joined the Lutheran Church in the community next to us. I became interested in civic affairs and worked with a neighborhood group on a big nationwide project. Essentially, we were fighting to implement the Princeton Plan in our school system. I became a neighborhood leader for CORE.

Chapter Five

I was beginning to enjoy my life. My new neighbors and connections kept creating committees, and I joined wherever I felt would benefit the children. One of Bill's younger brothers came to live with us as a teenager. One day, I was talking to him about colleges he could attend after graduating high school. It was then I realized I had talked about college with such passion, and I still wanted to go to college. I could not hide it anymore!

At the same time, Nassau Community College opened its first semester of Community College for Nassau County residents. It was reasonably priced at $10 a credit. I signed up for three courses in the Fall of 1962.

I had graduated from Julia Richman HS 10 years ago and had lost track of so many of my high school friends who had gone on to fulfill their college ambitions. I was not going to wait any longer. I decided that I would do the two-year program at Nassau Community College and then transfer to Hofstra University in Garden City and get my bachelor's.

I must confess that much of what I was thinking in my head came from various conversations I had had with my former classmates and people I met along the way. I had not gone to any college counselors that could help me make decisions. I was ready, though! I was bursting at the seams.

The year after I began at Nassau Community College, Bill enrolled as a student. I was so happy–at least in the beginning. Yet, he allowed himself to be dependent on me. I had my homework, and he wanted me to write all his essays. Why?? Not because he couldn't but because he was always busy. And as a wife, I should do it he must have felt. I did help him even though I wanted him to understand what college was all about. He passed the first year with high grades, especially in Composition and Math, of course.

The following year, he dropped out. He said it wasn't for him. When I asked him to help me with my math, he refused, stating he did not have the time. He had money to make, and if I wanted to stay in school, I could, but it was not for him. Living with Bill, one never knew what to expect because he loved "things."

One day in the late evening, I got a call from the Suffolk County police on Long Island Sound. I found out it had to do with my children being in a boat accident with their father, Bill, on his boat! They asked could I come and get them? Of course, I would come and get them; I was just trying to understand how and why my children were on a boat that supposedly my husband owned.

Needless to say, I was very upset and didn't know what to expect. Bill was becoming a wheeler and dealer. In exchange for work he had done, we owned a six sleeper passenger boat. He had hit one of the beams for the overhead bridge lightly, and the boat had a little damage. The children were a little shook up but there was no severe damage to anyone or the boat.

When I got home with my husband, I was more than angry. Need I say more? A year or two later, once we learned more about navigating the boat on Long Island Sound, we did have some very happy days on it as a fam-

Chapter Five

ily. It was an expense. He had to pay for it to be put up in the Freeport Marina, which was near where we lived.

In our house, in our recreation room, we had a jukebox, among other things, the old style that played 78rpm records in it. Bill loved having people come in for the jukebox. We also had a pinball machine and big swings in the backyard. We had the best female black Labrador that ever lived.

Yet it wasn't me at all; all the stuff. We worked hard every summer to have the best lawn. Even my dog Greco knew about the importance of the lawn. We had so many things because of Bill. Most of the time, my whole world had to go through Bill.

Bill showed films in our playroom. We had five large fish tanks with black mollies, big goldfish, and you name it. Bill had a special motor to run the five tanks and keep the water clean.

The music he played in our playroom had stereo speakers in the trees surrounding our house. He was well known for his music. He deejayed many events. I seriously needed to talk about my feelings and how I felt about everything. We never ate to our standard of living.

We had a pantry food budget but no real travel excursion dollars in our budget to fill what was the excitement of life for me. Over the years, I drove a Cadillac, a Chevy Impala, and a Buick Roadmaster. The cars were a surprise. I would go to drive the car we had, and it would be replaced by something else I wasn't expecting.

Whatever the kids were involved in had to have long-term planning. My mother bought her own home eventually; she needed her own integrity and power. She moved about 15 minutes away but was still in Nassau County. The kids could get to see her by riding their bikes to her when I couldn't take them.

She was much closer to bus, rail travel, and other conveniences that could help her be as mobile as she wanted to be. She also was able to meet new friends in that area. She was satisfied and happy to be more independent despite still not driving.

I had finally gotten the job-of my heart working with in Rockville Center for the New York Telephone Company. I had waited ten years going through repeated application processes and interviews in New York City and Nassau County. They had rejected me at least five times.

In 1953, after graduating from Julia Richman HS, I wanted to work as a business representative for a telephone company in New York. It was their highest-level job, and I wanted to do that. I met all kinds of obstacles and blocks. Over a 10-year period I applied seven times. I was rejected all seven times for various reasons that were obviously pointing to the same reason, my skin color.

As my mother used to say, "Persistence is my middle name." It was one of their highest-paying positions for a female employee during that time. I trained for three weeks for the position. I love the position, and felt very fulfilled with it.

Chapter Five

By the time I got the position, I had a year and a half left before I got my bachelor degree. It was very interesting that for three of the interviews that I went on for the job over several years, I was told I had to have at least full years of college or an AA degree. When I went to work in my office, out of 46 girls, there were only three of us with college credit!

In my job at the New York telephone company, I was part of the office staff of 40 who were invited to a celebration and promotion for one of the managers. The party was in the evening from 6 to 9 off of Long Beach Long Island. It was a very dressed-up affair, and it was very cold that night, so people left the party individually. I had driven myself and was not familiar with the area at all because it was off of the ocean or nearby, and I wasn't familiar with Long Beach.

I understood that the area was a bit wealthy and pretentious. When I left the party, I did something that probably wasn't the smartest thing. I sat in the car and let the engine heat up with the radiator on high to get some heat. It was a darkened area.

When I took off and went a few feet, I hit something pretty hard, and my head hit the side glass window. I was dazed and stayed like that for a few minutes until the police car came. They went around the car and, looked at my injury, asked me some questions, to which I answered. Yes, I slurred a little, but my lip was swollen.

They advised me they were taking me to the small police station. They would do follow up on me to find out where I was coming from. I explained as well as I could but let them know I was on my way home.

They arrested me! Not for hitting anything, but a suspicion. I'm sure they didn't believe I was in a high profile community from a party in the late evening. It was 10pm and I was dressed to the hilt as I was in high heels and a very beautiful black cocktail dress. They did not believe I was an invitee.

I had to be arraigned in the court the following morning. I spent an evening in a cold jail cell. Early the next morning, I found out that it was serious. The matron explained to me it did not look good for me. I really didn't know or understand what she was talking about at the time.

I asked her if I could call my boss and get him to explain why I was at the party. I also told her I was a college student and my position at the New York telephone company's office in Rockville Center. When I explained to her, she said, "Well, you better make sure you tell that to the attorney that they have assigned to you." At the courthouse prior to the arraignment, I followed her instructions and was then directed to go with my attorney into a special conference room in the courthouse. I was beginning to feel very nervous.

My husband was waiting in the courtroom for me. I had seen him, but my attorney told me to wait there until he came to me. He advised my husband to be patient. I had no other choice but to see what the judge would rule. I had been injured on the side of my lip, so my lip was slightly swollen, and I did look a bit ridiculous in heels

Chapter Five

and a black cocktail dress. Soon,, the judge came in.

I told him my story. The judge looked at me and smiled. He said, "I know you were there because I was there, and I saw you on the floor dancing. And, young lady, you were pretty good." He excused my attorney and the other matron. He explained that I would be released.

There was a waiver for me to sign not charging the arresting officer. He also said that since they could not detect what I had hit, they would investigate that. My level of humiliation was as big as a sky balloon. I had to go to my workplace and explain what happened to my manager.

There was hardly a time in my life when I couldn't use extra money. As I planned for my first Caribbean trip, I needed some dental work, so I took a Short term part-time cleaning job on Saturday mornings. One day, the homeowner, who was a New York City "schoolteacher," was there as I worked. Her son was there also. We got into a brief conversation about his college studies since we both were going to Hofstra University.

When she noticed us talking, she asked him about our conversation. He explained to his mother I was also a student at Hofstra University. A few weeks later, she explained to me she would not hire me again because she wanted just a housemaid, not a "college housemaid." In a very non-confrontational way, I explained to her, I had no intention of returning since I took the job only short term. I was not humiliated, just saddened.

In August of 1965, I got the opportunity to travel

on a 4 day 3 night trip with my good friend to St. Thomas, Virgin Islands. I still had neurodermatitis breakouts, and I had learned that it was due to nerves. My inability to relax. My friend's husband had been in the military and stationed in St. Thomas. He always talked about how much he loved being there. My mother agreed to take care of the kids for the weekend.

I had to get away from school and responsibilities for even a 4 day 3 night holiday to St. Thomas. For the first time, I saw San Juan, Puerto Rico and the first time, I saw St. Thomas, Virgin Islands, it was August 1965. I think I got hooked. It was like an Essence magazine photo spread.

I smiled 24 hours daily, even during sleep. My spirit was infused, and in this case, appearances were not deceiving. I had a great weekend. I was surprised by the circumstances as well as someone who was going to help me turn my life around. My struggles and my setbacks were now moving in a different direction.

Was this going to be part of God's plan for my life? This meeting with Tony from my perspective was not a setback but a move forward. In every picture I took of smiling faces, I saw a future for myself that I couldn't fully grasp.

I returned to New York on a high. Bill's life was becoming complicated and he had his 3rd child on the way. I was not pregnant and we agreed to actively participate in preparing for our challenges and changes.

I returned to St. Thomas for a 5-day visit from

Chapter Five

New Year in 1966. Through connections, I was unable to secure a position working for VITELCO in St. Thomas, but I was given a 6-week position with VITELCO in St Croix.

I returned to St Thomas in July of 1966 to work for six weeks for VITELCO in St. Croix. I took the Seaplane from St. Thomas every morning and returned from St Croix to St. Thomas every afternoon at 4:30 PM. WHAT A SUMMER! I got prepared for what could be possible. I was going to leave the old behind and be in uncertainty about my future. How was such an appointment possible?

I was hired based on my excellent credentials from the New York Telephone Company in Rockville Center. I also inquired about teaching in St. Thomas. The Assistant Comm of Commerce, Mr. Darwin Creque, promised to send me an application for employment with the Virgin Islands Department of Education for the school year 1967.

I recognized that my life had a lot of purpose in New York, but I felt I had to make a change. I was moving from my house. My friends, family members, and loved ones were concerned for me.

I couldn't really grasp for myself what I wanted to do, but my foresight told me a change was necessary. Bill had put himself in a relationship with a child on the way. I was concerned about the potential for me and my two children. I knew I had to be able to give them a solid future.

One more year before I would graduate and earn my Bachelor of Arts in Social Studies. My degree was my motivation. My mother had to agree to help, to be my support, or I knew I could not be complete for my very own transformation. It was extraordinary that she was agreeable, if not overjoyed, and she was going to help me.

She had met "Tony" on the phone many times, and he was going to come to New York to meet my children, my mother, close family and friends before the move. My mother began to help me with prayer and more prayer. My faith helped me to have hope. Would the great and friendly smile be enough motivation for this new possibility? He was waiting for me "to come back to the Virgin Islands." What to do? What to do?

Martin Luther King Jr. said, "Faith Is taking the first step even when you don't see the whole staircase."

Chapter Six

The Whole Staircase

I was committed to going to the St Thomas Carnival celebration in April 1967. Tony and I had decided to make our relationship serious, and we made plans for another return to Saint Thomas during the Carnival before I moved there. He said, "That would be the time to come back and spend a fun time with me. I can't describe how much fun the Carnival will be for you, especially if it's your first time. So I want you to come.

I decided that I would go …even his buddies wanted me to come and said, "You will have fun." I couldn't resist, and at 32, I felt it was what I needed. The music was fantastic. I particularly remember a calypso song that was played over and over again. It was out of Trinidad and trendy, "Fire, fire in your wire." And dancing to that song, the steel pan, and tramping in the streets was unbelievable!!

Unbelievably, in April of 1967, it was so safe! I was with Tony, my new everything. Yes, we were in love, and he made sure that I had the best time ever!

I saw my first moko jumbies! They are the parade stilt walkers… but in a different sense than you would see them in or outside the Caribbean islands, mainly Saint Thomas. They could dance on one leg. They could hold up one leg and dance, as well as dance with you standing on the ground level. They stood seven or eight feet tall. That day, it was parade day when I saw them.

The parade day was fantastic. More than I could have imagined, it was filled with the local people in their troupes, with outstanding costumes. You could not imagine the costumes.

These costumes were worked on for months and months during the year. Many of the troupes had more than 100 or more members of the community from various businesses and organizations, and they all danced to the music. I had been transformed…I was ready to move!

I had read about Magen's Bay before I saw Saint Thomas in a National Geographic magazine. It was described as one of the ten most beautiful beaches in the world. The parties at the gorgeous Magen's Bay beach after Carnival were fantastic.

The food and the music were so good. There was no charge for the food and drinks. Even now, almost 60 years later, I can still see and feel the free spirit within me that enjoyed the sun, the sand, and the sea. It all promised me a new life.

The history of the Carnivals in St. Thomas de-

Chapter Six

serves an entire book. Millions have traveled to St.Thomas since my initial visit and kept Carnival alive in their heart. Tony kept it alive for me right down to getting me safely on my flight back to New York. He loaded my carry-on bag with a gift of my favorite island foods, patays, and coconut tarts. I slept happily on my return flight back to New York to JFK Airport.

I remember believing my change and joy would be centered around the two of us. The love, the glow, and the fire between us endured many setups and setbacks right down to the very end of life;I have no regrets. Yet I would come to see that my move to St Thomas was about more than a 48-year love affair. I am blessed to still have memories.

Because of an error in my Social Studies course requirements, which I did not realize until it was too late to correct, I had to take one two-credit course in the summer of 1967. I missed walking down the aisle for my June graduation, but it was just "life happening." Tony decided to come to New York to meet my family and friends.

My mother and I had come to a mutual understanding about my leaving for Saint Thomas and settling there for my future. Additionally, that understanding was about having her grandchildren return every summer to visit her and their Dad. I explained I would also come with them.

She seemed alright with it. Many of my friends could not understand why I would make such a move. Not only my friends but also many of my relatives who were close to me. Needless to say, they tried to talk me out of it, but I was sure I was making the right move.

Tony usually called me every day from St. Thomas. I could never understand how. Sometimes, when he called me to see if friends or family were nearby, he also spoke to them. My friends and family were beginning to feel more reassured that I would be OK in my new home 1,700 miles from New York.

I let everyone know that since I was on the list of new hires for the Department of Education, I would have holidays and summers off. Everyone said, "We're coming to visit!" Tony reassured them all that they would be welcomed. Bill and I communicated, and he had been resistant to the move but finally agreed that on the small island of St. Thomas and its simplicity, the kids would be better off with me.

Denise was almost 10 years old, and Lester was almost 15 years old. Bill would be a support for the children at my mother's house until I sent for them in October 1967. We needed an apartment in town in St Thomas within walking distance of the schools that would be accommodating for the four of us.

Tony came to visit me the last week of June. My mother, who had been married to two Caribbean men, became very fond of him. He could cook the dishes she loved, and he was so handy around the house that he even ironed for her and told her to relax. With his winning smile, he could have sold her the Brooklyn Bridge.

One of my cousins liked him very much, and they hit it off right away. My play brother JR, who met him,

Chapter Six

said, "Don't go all the way down there. I'll find you a boyfriend if that is what this is all about." It was nothing to debate, though; I was ready to leave New York.

My letter came from the Virgin Islands Department of Education the next day, and it indicated that I had been assigned to the Charlotte Amalie High School in Saint Thomas, United States Virgin Islands, as a Social Studies teacher for Grades 9 through 12. I was to report on Thursday, August 31st, 1967, and school would begin on Tuesday, September 5th, 1967. Charlotte Amalie High School was only a 5-minute walk away from the Caribbean Sea and from what was to be my classroom, room 212. Looking out the classroom door or walking the corridor was a nice picturesque view of the Caribbean Sea, and often, six large cruise ships would be docked. Often, millionaires' yachts were sailing in and out of the harbor.

You could not get a much better view than that each and every day. Monday through Friday, 8:20 AM to 3:00 PM, which is what I got used to looking at, and I loved it. I thought my new life would begin when I got off the plane in Saint Thomas on August 8th, 1967. My people-to-people world would begin in the classroom, the hallways, and the byways of Charlotte Amalie High School. With my heart filled with hope and my mind a little overwhelmed, I said a silent prayer to my Heavenly Father for His divine guidance.

I was leaving a community of neighbors, families, and friends in New York and Nassau County because the demographics in both areas were static, keeping the door open for more disappointments. The demographics of 1967 in St. Thomas, US Virgin Islands, had shifted in my favor. They needed teachers, and apparently, they needed me.

I liked to believe they wanted me because I was a graduate of Julia High School and Hofstra University. I came with good academic skills and with the motto of Charlotte Amalie HS, "To Excel Always." I was the right person to teach Social Studies classes. The first day of school for teachers and the first day of the rest of my life was an experience to be treasured.

My Love

PRE
TTY
OLD
A film by
WALTER MATTESON

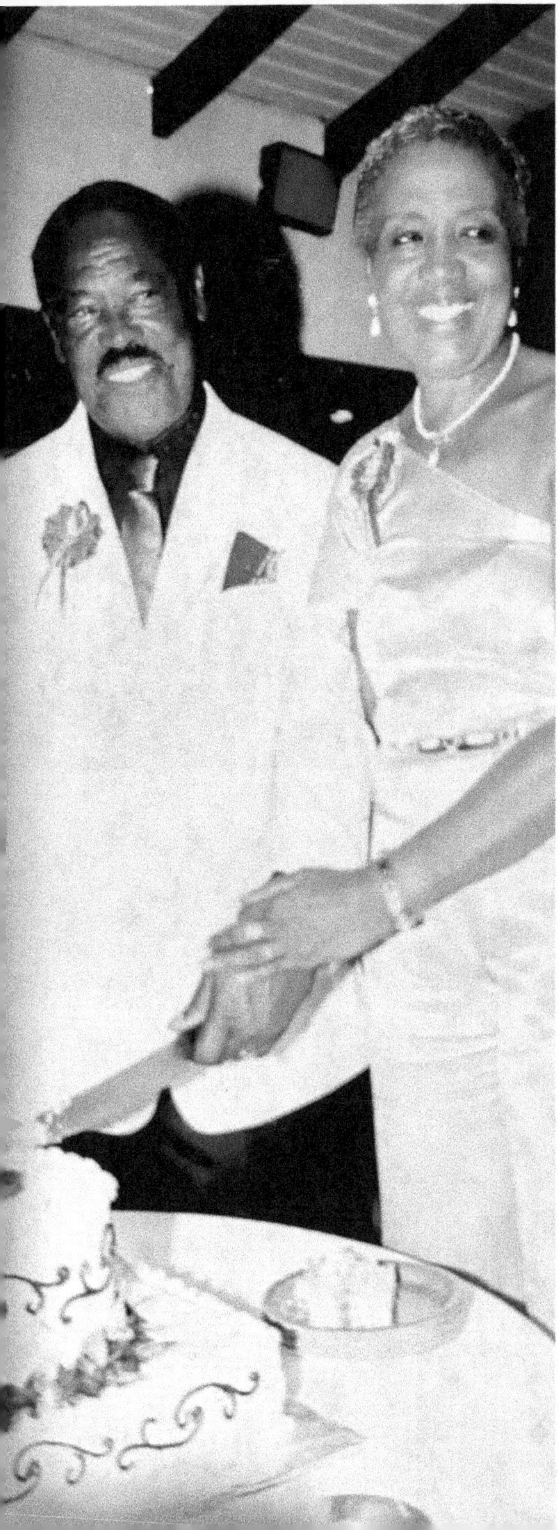

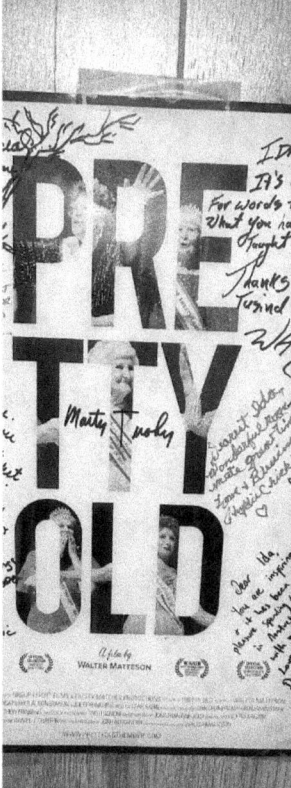

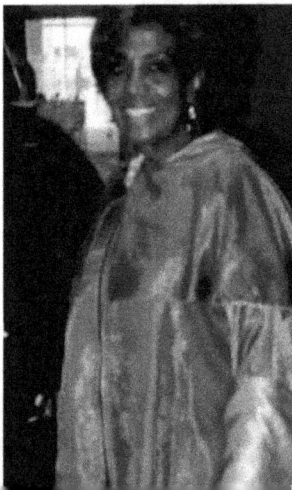

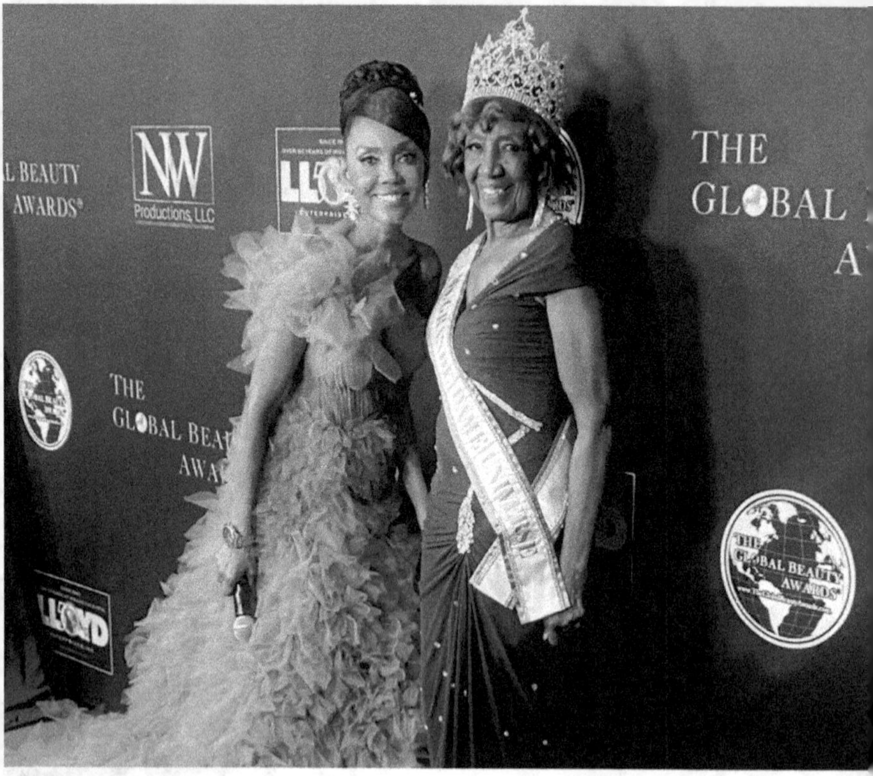
NW
Productions, LLC
THE
GLOBAL
THE GLOBAL BEAUTY AWARDS

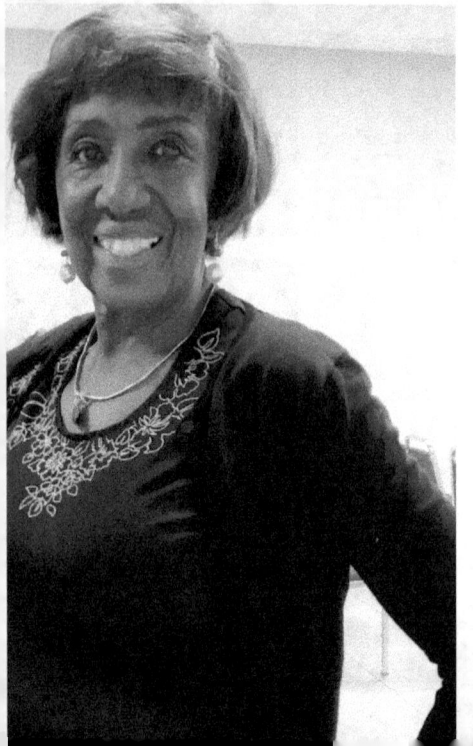

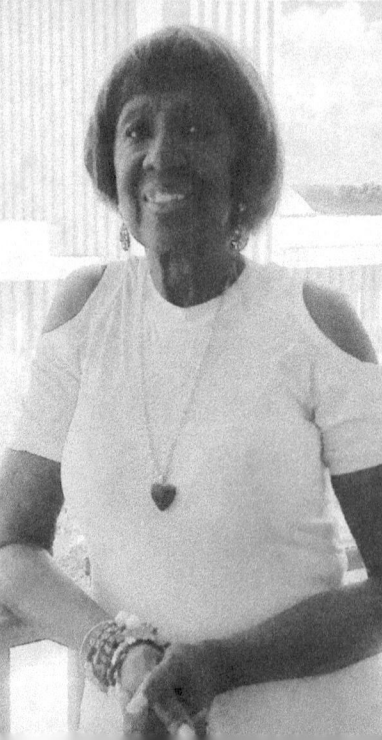

Chapter Seven

The Heart of My St. Thomian Experiences and Legacy at Charlotte Amalie School

It was the first day of the rest of my life and an experience to be treasured. The Charlotte Amalie High School bell was ringing loudly. Students in navy blue and light blue were everywhere. I was walking fast and remembered I had to go up the front set of stairs to go to the office to sign in. The students were in the way, and I kept thinking, "Stay calm, Ida." Finally, I arrived at the office and was able to sign in. Now, the students seem to be going towards their classrooms. Some teachers were passing and smiling at me, but I was so out of breath from running that I could barely nod in their direction.

The new principal passed by me in a hurry on his way to the office. Thank God he did not look my way as I reached room 212 just as the second bell rang. The classroom was half full of empty desks, with many students rushing past me to their seats. As I put my stuff on the desk and turned to face the class, I took a deep breath and smiled at them.

It seemed as if there were about 25 boys and girls shined up and pretty sparkling in their powder blue shirts and navy pleated skirts or navy trousers, white socks, and black shoes. The girls had nice hairdos and the boys had haircuts. I was impressed because they were 9th graders. They were quiet as they looked me up and down. One student yelled out, "You are tall teacher. How tall are you?"

I introduced myself, and I realized I had 21 students: thirteen males and eight females. As I spoke, some of them still continued to talk to each other. The young male students decided to sit in the front row and stare at me. Finally, they got quiet. I didn't have to say "quiet" to get them to hush. I didn't know if I should sit or stand (Fashion-wise, at this time, pants were not part of the women's dress code).

Female teachers wore pantyhose or stockings, and since the boys were staring, I wondered if I had a run in my stocking. Thank God the bell rang because it was a short period day. One of the students said, " See you later, Teach." I thought I should remind him that I was Missus White to him, so I did.

He just smiled and kept walking through the door. That was how my first day went. At our department meeting, I met some of my fellow teachers, and we shared our experiences. Three of us were brand new. I was the only one from the United States; the others were recent graduates from a university stateside, but they were Virgin Islanders.

My department chairperson was someone who

Chapter Seven

had lived in Saint Thomas for many years. She was okay. However, Mrs. Mary Francis, a seasoned educator in heart and spirit, was so supportive and helpful to me on my teaching journey. She and I shared the same birth date, April 12.

She was to be my rock, my strength, and was always there for me and my family as well. She also lived around the corner from me, and she let me know that she was always there if I needed her. My goodness, she was a one-of-a-kind. I will always be grateful to her. "Hallelujah! Thank you, Lord, for bringing her into my life."

My First Homeroom, 9-3 to 12-3, CAHS Class of 1971

With the homeroom assigned to me as I entered as a new teacher from the mainland of the United States, I was a target for many potential things that could happen to me. Yet that did not happen at all with my homeroom. Each of them had their own characteristic in the homeroom classroom.

They were leaders in their school in academics, sports, school government, and community service. They held and respected the school motto, "to excel always." What a joy it was to be their homeroom teacher! What a joy it is to still be in touch with some of them through social media.

The CAHS Social Studies Department

We had no equal anywhere! Within our department during my time there of eight years, we had 8 to 10 social studies teachers. Our backgrounds were diverse because some of the teachers were from St. Thomas, Virgin Islands, and some were from the mainland here and there.

For example, I had the opportunity to collaborate with the department chairperson, Mrs. Mary Francis. We initiated a very innovative project to support students who, upon graduation from Charlotte Amalie High School, could get a grant or financial assistance.

We eventually gave up to 5 scholarships in the amount of $500.00 each. I initially went to Puerto Rico and was able to get various types of candy bars and other snacks for sale during the lunch hour and class transition. I went to Puerto Rico for the first school year, and we sold until we were able to get the same costs in St. Thomas.

The project went on for many years and assisted many students with financial grants. Mary Francis and her leadership inspired us all to be the best we could be. She opened my eyes to all that I could be.

As a social studies teacher, I have always found the UN and its operating procedures very interesting. As a young student in New York City, I remember when the United Nations building was completed. I visited the site as part of a field trip and was amazed at its objectives for humanity everywhere. So, as a CAHS Social Studies, I was able twice to take advantage of taking students to Rami Air Force Base in Puerto Rico to be part of the model United Nations activity for HS students. The experience was awesome for me and the students as they participated and were able to view global concerns from a

Chapter Seven

different perspective.

The CAHS Guidance Counselors Department
After eight years as a social studies teacher, I was able to move into a much-loved area that I felt called to. I became a Guidance Counselor. As a CA HS Guidance Counselor, you started with the 9th grade class and remained with them through 12th grade.

As a guidance counselor, my involvement with students and their four years through CAHS allowed me to be their advocate inside and outside of CAHS. It was such a broad spectrum that I found myself in many community and education-related support groups. For six years, I was appointed to the Virgin Vocational Advisory Board, which took me to meetings monthly in St. Thomas, St. Croix, and St. John. I supported many valid ideas for positive change or maintenance of Vocational Education in the territory.

One such program that I became aware of as a Social Studies teacher and then as a Guidance Counselor at Charlotte Amalie High School was Civil Air Patrol. The Civil Air Patrol program met every Saturday at the airport in St. Thomas. I was recruited by the local commander, Senator Eric Freeman.

He was the Captain of the newly formed squadron, which would be under Puerto Rico. He approached me and asked me to be a volunteer. I agreed to train for the position of Aerospace Educator (once he explained to me what the demands would be). After my training was completed, I became our Second Lt. Aerospace Education Officer.

My role was to work with cadets and see that they completed workbook assignments. In addition, as the Aerospace Education Officer, I often went on my own to Puerto Rico sites to fulfill and expedite the tasks of getting uniforms for new cadets. Over the years, I went to Fort Buchanan for various activities as needed. Several of us held various official leadership titles.

I flew in helicopter copters with and without students. I also took two flying lessons, which I ended abruptly. My heart fluttered too much. Eventually, when I was promoted to Ist Lt., I traveled to the US mainland Air Force Base in full dress uniformed as 1st Lt Ida White, Aerospace Education Officer, with our new Commander.

We were entitled to eat in the Officer Clubs. We were so proud of our Drill team. We went throughout the USVI with the Drill team for many, many parades. I remained a faithful and proud member of our Civil Air Patrol Squadron for seven years.

More projects and activities that shaped my journey.

For almost 10 years, I worked in Adult Education as a counselor. I also worked at Fort Christian prison, where I tested prisoners at the Adult Basic level so they could get into adult education at high school. I am so very happy that adult education training is a part of my educational background because it brings a great level of satisfaction. When I think of being involved in school and community and making a difference to those who need to take some extra steps to make themselves whole, it is very rewarding.

Chapter Seven

Aside from my involvement with education activities because of my position as a social studies teacher and a guidance counselor, community service was a major part of my life. This was not just for students; the overall community needs were a part of my overall interest. I was the Career Education Specialist for St. Thomas, and I worked in Adult Education programs in the community with the VI Police Department and the Prison system for a couple of years. I served for two years as the Alternative Education Coordinator and six years as the Student Services Coordinator for the territory.

Projects That Were Life Changing

During this period of time, I met someone who helped me get very focused. I held many titled positions, and without question, under the artful leadership of our 8-year Commissioner of Education, Dr. Linda Creque, I was successful. I could not have done it without the help of a very talented, dedicated, and hard-working staff. We were able to implement innovative initiatives, both local and federal, throughout the territory from the Office of Student Service.

As Coordinator, I had the benefit of meeting a delightful lady, Dr. Virgie Binford from the US Department of Education, who was on loan to the Virgin Islands for a year. She became my mentor up to her death several years ago. She helped me to successfully bridge the gap between ambition and achievement.

Dr. Binford had heard me give my presentation on the life of Sojourner Truth in the library in St. Thomas for Black History Week the previous year. The following year, when she returned to Richmond, Virginia, she spoke to me several months in advance of Black History Month and asked me if I would come to Richmond and give the presentation. I agreed to do it.

After putting on my costume that evening, I clearly remember hearing her at the mic. I thought to myself, "I can't do this." My brain had frozen; I couldn't remember anything, and I said, "Oh my goodness, I can't do it." I don't remember anything.

However, the angel on the other side of my shoulder said you cannot disappoint Dr. Binford; she has given you a very beautiful introduction. The guests are awaiting you. You're from the Virgin Islands, you are representing the Virgin Islands, and you will do it! Yes, I did it then and many times since then.

That evening, it came off beautifully. It was a 20-minute presentation, and I only forgot one line. No one knew the difference.

Dr. Binford, who had traveled the world, took me with her to Hawaii, where we did a joint presentation on Career Education. When we had a similar education conference in St. Thomas for entertainment, I did 10 minutes of "stand-up" comedy. (I was funny in the daytime.) Dr. Binford encouraged me to do it there, also. I did and got laughs.

I began to observe and use this thought as a motivator. In life, you can pretty much be who you wish to be. You should, therefore, want to be someone of value…and who knows how far it can take you.

Chapter Seven

After her year with the VI Department Of Education, Dr. Binford continued to advise me as a soror. During her time in St. Thomas, she helped get the graduate sorority for Alpha Kappa Alpha organized and encouraged me to join. I did follow through, of course. Additionally, through her guidance and direction, I studied and earned a doctorate from two online schools, La Salle University in Slidell, Lousiana 1993 and in 2008, New Hope Bible Seminary 2012*.

Being a radio talk show host on a major radio station in St. Thomas was one of my best experiences. I hosted a weekly half-hour radio talk show entitled and "Educators Notebook" on WSTA for five years. Initially, it was my show with my ideas on education topics. But after a year or so on WSTA and broadcasting weekly, I had my education commissioner, Dr. Creque as a guest. She was so pleased with the outcome that she asked me if I would be interested in having education leaders or visitors to the island who were education officials be on my show. I was more than happy to be given such an opportunity, and I was pleased that I had earned her trust.

After five years, I was offered an hour-long talk show on WVWI, and I was able to expand a little further. The title of the show was "Issues and Ideas with Ida." it was a fun opportunity to test my abilities as a talk show host for an hour, but I have to say, at that time, it almost wore me out. I was still fully employed, and I continued working with the radio for a while until 2012.

I must share that I was an active Rotarian for more than 10 years with the Rotary II Club of St. Thomas. The Tattler" was our weekly Rotary II newsletter. I was editor for approximately 3 years, and I was assisted by Rotarian, S. Michele Downes. My big accomplishment that was very challenging but was an awesome activity for four years was cooking single-handedly every six weeks for the homeless and the hungry at our local Community Shelter. I loved the challenge!

You never knew what you were going to have to cook. Often, when it was chicken or ground meat, it was frozen when I got there. My job was to defrost it, cook it, and get the side items cooked to be ready for the hungry and the homeless by noon time.

I served as a mentor for many students from our Rotary attached school, Addelita Cancryn JHS. I still communicate with a few of them personally. I was our club's Rotarian of the Year and won other noteworthy awards. For 3 years, I was our Rotary Club's Sergeant at Arms, raising money in many fun ways. I even tried a couple of times to be an auctioneer. I guess I was successful because the items were sold.

Being a member of Rotary II was one of my "most unequaled experiences!" At the time, because I was an on-call employee with FEMA, I never made myself available for the position of President. I'm sad about that, but it was always understood that I had to recognize the priorities.

The Sheer Magic of Imagination Coming Live
I had a best girlfriend in St. Thomas, who shared so many ideas that I had and was such a great friend. We did so many things together and had so much fun putting them together in St. Thomas and Europe. She was just the best

Chapter Seven

of the best. She has passed away, but I cannot overlook how we began our friendship.

She liked to dance, and I liked to dance to Caribbean music. We noticed that many of our visitors to the island and the particular hotel that we went to were rotary, and many of the guests could benefit from Caribbean dance lessons. So we went to the hotel management in charge of such things at the Frenchman's Reef.

We explained that we could hold a class weekly for the guests and teach them how to dance, reggae, calypso, etc. On Tuesday nights, the nightclub played steelpan music. Two days after our meeting, we were given the OK and the date to begin. It was almost hilarious because we were not dance teachers; we just loved to dance.

However, they were going to pay us $25 an hour, and we were to begin the following Tuesday, which was four days away, so we had to get ready for our show. I implemented the idea of teaching the dance steps and moves. If we had an audience that didn't want to dance, some would be judges, and by applause, they would choose the dancer who would win a bottle of local Cruzan rum. We were very successful.

Several weeks after we started, one guest sat with us and said you girls need to get costumes to dance in. So we got costumes, and we danced in costume! We were invited to sit and talk with guests who found us fascinating. I was the microphone person explaining and telling jokes, etc. I was even asked for my autograph, and of course, we were always asked by someone to take pictures with the guests. Management came often to check, and most of the time, we drew a full crowd in the club.

We developed a dance routine that we performed weekly for a year. We highlighted Caribbean dancing in the nightclub as an activity for guests at our largest hotel, Frenchman's Reef Hotel in St. Thomas. Growing this business started a trend that all the hotels started to follow when we transitioned out of the market.

Life for me in St. Thomas was often so much more than a casual or an ordinary day. It was usually sheer magic. I played tennis; I ran the waterfront in the mornings. I went snorkeling often, and Tony had a community of friends with boating ties. So when we sailed and anchored, I could sometimes jump off the boat if Tony was there for fun swims.

Yes, the best days of my life were in St. Thomas, where I lived like a star! There were so many great days, and of course, there were sad days and sad weeks. Some of my worst days, in many ways, had to do with just being human and dealing with the humanness of people. I struggled and then learned, like the "woman at the well," to hold on and keep my faith, talk to the Lord, and get to know Him... But that is another book.

Tony and I were able to attend the Sinbad Soul Music Festival series. The first festival was held on French Saint Martin, Tony's Home Island, and aired on HBO in 1995. We had so much fun, and we were actually seen on HBO throughout the country every day of that series when there was a musical performance. Earth Wind &Fire, Gladys Knight, Frankie Beverly, and Tina Marie.

Chapter Seven

We got more than a dozen calls from friends who saw us. In 1999, when the festival came to St. Thomas, there were top artists like Chaka Khan and Smokey Robinson. My cousins, Frances and Alvin, joined us in St. Thomas for the fun and the great sounds of music. Those were such fun times.

Winning the crown of Ms. USVI Senior America in 1999 propelled me into 23 years of senior "beauty pageantry," and I say beauty not because of outer beauty as a senior woman but because of the glow of the true essence of inner beauty. I'm seeing hundreds of beautiful senior Queens, so I do not negate their beauty. However, we, as seniors, say beauty that comes from within gives you a beautiful heart and a beautiful smile. My cousins Francis and Alvin threw me a big party to celebrate my win. Those were awesome days, and it was great for Tony (the smile) and me because we traveled whenever we were invited to a destination, and it was just awesome.

Aspirations and Travel

I did not grow up in the Virgin Islands, but while living there, I had a distinct interest in everything Virgin Islands. I was so excited when I was able to take a three-week graduate study tour with the University of Pittsburgh that involved graduate study evaluation coursework in Denmark with trips to Sweden and Norway. Since our main class work was done in Copenhagen, I got a chance to visit the museum in Copenhagen that featured so many items donated by individuals from the Saint Thomas Virgin Islands. Many of whom were names that I recognized.

I ended up spending five weeks in Europe, traveling to Sweden and Norway during that trip because I went a week before the graduate class began and stayed a week after it ended. Oh my goodness, it was one of the best times I ever had in travel. Once I learned that European summer study programs provided safety as well as European travel, I took other coursework during the summer and visited so many countries in Europe.

To my surprise, when working on my first doctorate with my very good friend, Dr. Martha Herby (a VI resident at that time), we presented a paper related to the Virgin Islands in Dubrovnik, Yugoslavia. We got a standing ovation. It was this opportunity that created my desire to complete doctoral studies, even if I did it online.

The paper was later published in an Organizational Development journal. A few months later, my good friend Dr. Eddy Donahue had a copy mailed to him in St. Thomas by his colleague in Europe since it was properly noted that we were from the US Virgin Islands. It was awesome to see our name printed as speakers in Dubrovnik.

MY Reflections, MY Memories, My Musings

My hope was to live forever with Tony in St. Thomas.Then one day without a whole lot of planning and preparation, it became evident that 47 years of living in St. Thomas US Virgin Islands with my love, my love train with Tony was coming to an end. In all honesty, our dedication to each other, the many island escapades, and happenings demands its own novela."

Chapter Seven

Tony, nee Antonio, was essential to helping me develop the " Ida personality and the Ms. White personality" for my students. I often referred to Tony as Mr. Personality because of his smile and friendliness. He knew everyone on the island. He also had the kind of charm that emerged from inside of him that wasn't learned from any techniques or behaviors.

Women, men, and children loved him. He had that male French charm coming from the French island of St. Martin. I loved that kind of charm that was missing from my early life. Laughter is so necessary at the "right times."

Tony and I raised our children together for many years in St. Thomas. Affluent in French, Tony also spoke Spanish and Dutch. Together, we were able to travel to St Martin and nearby islands, numerous times visiting family and friends and making new ones.

Additionally, we traveled near and far together and even went to his home, St. Martin. We even had a timeshare on the Dutch side of St. Maarten, where we went sometimes just to hide out. During those years of running a home together, we had many challenges, especially hurricane weather, that fostered concerns about our safety.

Yet Tony supported me in my efforts to grow academically. I went on to gain my Master's degree from the University of The Virgin, a Doctorate from La Salle University in Slidell, Louisiana, and a Doctorate in Bible studies from New Hope Seminary in Baltimore, Maryland.

It HAPPENED TO ME...
PROSE POEM
BY Dr. Ida White

In 1493... as Columbus sailed the seas, he
spied a chain of islands oh so heavenly.. and nice
He thought he'd found paradise
So, Signor Columbus planted the Spanish flag &
As well... to honor ST. URSULA & HER 11,00
beautiful VIRGINS,
He called the islands,   Virgin Islands,
By 1644, 4 more flags had flown, bringing
Buccaneers & She pirates ashore.
Selling rum and stolen goods to any store
By 1671,   the DANENBORG flew & Denmark came
up with a plan to grow
Sugarcane is a major cash flow,
By 1864, their sugar cash flow went dead!
"Sell them islands," Denmark said!   "We'll buy,"
the US said!
By 1917, the 3 Danish Virgin Islands finally became
the 3 US Virgin Islands.
For the sale price of 25 million in gold
bullion..........OH JOY!!!!!!!

BY 1957, thousands, then later...millions ... came to the Virgins
For da sun, da sand, and da sea.
I know ...cause it happened to me ... IN, 1967, St Thomas, Virgin
Welcomed New Yorker Ida and her 2 children,
Spoiling dem with sunny days, blue-green seas, da sparkling sand,
 Steel bands, da mocko jumbies, dancing in da street, and Carnival!!!
Spiritual, positive ...and personal, young Ida followed Tony's call,
Yes... Sometimes she did crack meh, son ...but.. she always got her groove back
Now de time for Ida did com to shed her tears... to leave Tony was a whack
To leave de great fun...teaching, dancing, learning, meeting and alla dat
Thankin you, Lord, for islands so nice...I thought I found paradise and all dat

Tony and I moved together from St Thomas in 2012 to Kissimmee, Florida, to combat Tony's aggressive dementia. We had had a rich, full life and remained together for 47 years until Tony passed away at age 79 on April 8, 2014. I was with him up to minutes before he passed, and Tony had acknowledged my presence and love for him by murmuring, "Thanks," seconds before his last breath. My dear cousin Liz was with me and felt that spiritual understanding of the last moments. The love that we had endured many obstacles and that love still remains.

Special Significance and Note:

In 1995, Hurricane Marilyn devastated St. Thomas, US Virgin Islands, just ten months after my official retirement from the Virgin Islands Department of Education.

I began work with FEMA as an Equal Rights Officer Reservist on call. A workforce of more than 800 persons was needed to restore the island. After ten years as an equal rights officer, part of my role was to train FEMA employees annually or when they were deployed.

Three courses that we offered were required to keep training up-to-date for employees, new and old. Those courses were related to equal rights without discrimination based on age, sex, national origin, race, or disability. Over the years, more indicators have been added. I began working with FEMA in October 1995 after Hurricane Marilyn devastated the island of St. Thomas.

The devastation was islandwide. We had no power, and the situation was so serious. They had to bring a

Chapter Seven

communication ship to the harbor so that the immediate needs for managing the island after such devastation could begin. I worked in that same position, traveling all over the US.

So many areas of the country have had devastation, and in many cases, disaster management is facilitated more easily when staff is trained. I have trained more than 10,000 staff repetitively as required for coursework. In 2008, I qualified as a certified Chief of Staff responsible for up to 300 persons in a declared disaster.

I retired from FEMA at age 83, a little more than 20 years after being hired in 1999. I contracted a viral infection in my heart at a disaster where I was subsequently hospitalized because of breathing viral air from within the office working area. My life as a FEMA employee traveling the country, being a part of management, meeting with community leaders and pastors, and providing information for disaster survivors was more than I could convey in a short period of time. There were many incidents that I will never forget.

However, I was deployed to Arkansas when President Clinton was making his last tour. Only a few hundred persons could get in the hangar at the airport. I was off in the afternoon and decided I would go to the hangar at the airport and shake the President's hand. I would write the article and submit it to the Daily News. I was a guest editorialist writing articles for the daily news, so I knew it would be OK to post myself in the daily news in St. Thomas, Virgin Islands.

It was a long time before the guest line for handshakes was formed. When President Clinton got to me and extended his hand to shake, he smiled and shook my hand. I did get a chance to see the blue eyes. He started to move along to the next person standing close to me. When I said to him, "I am from the Virgin Islands," he stopped and stepped back to me. He then asked me, "Which island?"

I said, "St. Thomas." He replied, "I love the Virgin Islands." His comment put a smile on both our faces. I was so cold after standing and waiting in the hangar for an hour and a half, but his response literally warmed my heart.

I worked 75 percent of all the major disasters during my 23 years, including 9/11 and Hurricane Katrina. Working with FEMA, I worked in two-thirds of all the fifty U.S. states, plus many deployments to Puerto Rico and my home area of the US VI (twice in St. Croix). When I lived in New York, I was aware of the beginning of the Ebony Fashion Fair models.

When they were beginning their search for tall, black, or dark-skinned models, I submitted my name and the paperwork to the agency, Ophelia DeVore, who was responsible for applications. I later learned that if you were accepted, you would be traveling, etc., etc. I had two children and had no intention of being in that kind of position. I thought that you would be taught how to do runway modeling. I withdrew my application, and they charged me a fee.

I was such an admirer of Naomi Sims. She was tall, dark-skinned, and beautiful. However, that was as

Chapter Seven

close as I ever came to thinking of myself as a contestant in a Senior pageant–before I did it!

Yet winning the crown of Ms. USVI Senior America in 1999 propelled me into 23 years of senior "beauty" pageantry. I say beauty not because of outer beauty as a senior but because of the representation of the true essence of inner beauty. I have seen hundreds of beautiful Senior queens, so I do not negate the beauty of Senior pageant contestants. However, we, as seniors, say beauty that comes from within gives you a beautiful heart and a beautiful smile.

In 2012, I starred in the award-winning documentary on senior pageants. "Pretty Old," directed by Walter Matteson and Sarah Jessica Parker, is still available on Amazon. For years, it was on Netflix and Hulu. This film stands as a classic, highlighting what senior pageants are all about from many viewpoints, especially the senior ladies. I'm the last remaining featured star alive, but I speak with other remaining cast members frequently, my besties Sharon M, Charlotte, and Carol.

I connect with Connie, especially on social media. Sadly, our leader and organizer of the Ms. Senior Sweetheart Pageant, Lennie Kaplan, passed away in recent years. Our Pretty Old film Director, Walter Matteson, stays in touch with me, as do others from the executive chair.

I won Ms. Senior Sweetheart/Int'l 2014, joining past US Virgin Island Queen winners Ms. Carol Tuohy and Ms. Toya Andrew in that history of wins. I was the last crowned winner for that title. We always loved performing together after my win as the three Virgin Queens in the St. Thomas and St. John nursing homes when the three of us were together.

I hold four other state crowns from Florida and designation titles: 1999 Ms. US Virgin Islands Senior Universe. In 2022, many-titled Ms. US Virgin Islands Senior. Also, Ms. US Virgin Islands Super Senior Universe and Ms. Grande Dame Universe.

In 2024, I added my support to the pageant group "Sparkle Nation Lifetime & Brand Ambassadors." I am still strengthened from within to continue to reach out to others in circumstances where they need my support.

> I have smiled way forever into US Virgin Islands history!!

The Global Beauty Awards 2022 in Seattle, Washington chose me from a highly competitive group of applicants for their "Most Impactful Award." In a competition of highly qualified applicants, the category chose the winner meeting the following qualities: "Having overcome hardship, continue to live victoriously, and they use their stories to uplift and encourage others." The win was such a dramatic win for me!

My "bestie" friend Sharon looked at my background and basically submitted the application. This will not die for me. It was awarded to me based on the" life chosen" for me to live and that I have lived to the best of my ability. It helped bring about real and lasting change in my heart, and that is why I have chosen to put it all out there.

Chapter Seven
IMPACTS & REFLECTIONS

"Tony's impact on my life is that wherever we are in God's heavenly realm, through our love, we will always find each other

Moving to Kissimmee, Florida, and later grieving over Tony for many years after his passing was overwhelming. My sadness continues still. Yet I was shocked that I could revisit the many places of fun, joy, and happiness that we shared, and I still love it so much. I survived. I also returned to St. Martin without him, and I survived. I often returned to St. Thomas without him (until Hurricane Maria destroyed my property there), but I survived that. I continued on, and I planted seeds in so many places.

I was a volunteer at Give Kids The World for 8 years, donating hundreds of hours annually. GKTW helped me to survive the desperation and the fear of loneliness. I volunteered in the gift shop for almost 8 years, and to me, I was the most awesome Fairy Godmother in entertainment during those four years! Lots of Sunday mornings, I rushed from church to make morning tea for our children and families. I also did evening events with a parade of princesses, princes, pirates, and vagabonds—such fun for the families as well as the characters.

I became one of the regular committee members. I was also a volunteer at KMS (Kissimmee Main Street), a business-based and history-based member. Even though I didn't have a brick-and-mortar business, my businesses are MLM-based. I'm welcome to contribute something. As a member for more than five years, we work towards our area's growth, revitalization, and growth on a history-based model. Each year, I had something locally for Black History Month.

In 2021, until the pandemic. I went to Dubai for a New Year's celebration to usher in 2022. How fabulous that was! Yet, I suffered unnecessary pain and even a walking disability because I hurt myself in a laughable way, trying to ride a camel. Yes, I kid you not at all. I have endured the pain, and now it is no longer a funny story.

I can't even talk about it anymore. Hope, though, is on my horizon. Remember, always "trust in the Lord with all your heart and lean not unto your own understanding. In all your ways acknowledge Him, and He will direct your path." My path is taking me on avenues of healing, and I am so grateful. So when I think about Dubai, the camel, and was it all worth it? Yes, it was!

In August 2022, I remember participating as a guest speaker at the UN Call to Action Intervention on Education as a guest presenter…from St Thomas.

In 2023, through WOLMII, as an assigned member of the committee focusing on Child Trafficking as an honored Peace Ambassador to the UN, I earned my badge and title. Currently, there is much to do as a global community, and even our tiny efforts add up to be worthwhile. In my mind, in our Lord's mind, we need to be careful of what we embrace and expose our hearts to. We must remember Philippians 4:7, "The peace of God which passeth all understanding will guard your hearts and minds through Christ Jesus."

Chapter Seven

Through WOLMI, I have worked with a committee of leaders from around the world on eradicating human trafficking and child trafficking. It is SDG 8.7 of the UN, and efforts to eradicate this evil from our world by 2030 are being worked on globally. We must keep the faith to be vigilant.

So many people ask me, why did I move to St. Thomas…to the Virgin Islands. Remember, way back, I, too, had questions for my Mom & Dad…that would never have verbal answers….. It seems like questions that make you confused abound. Answers are not always needed. Sometimes, looking for answers can diminish your spiritual strength. You have to discern. My friends, my life has been a life rich with experiences and contributions. I now can enjoy the joy. So now, I'm even more proud of the journey from 1935 until now.

Epilogue

Epilogue

In recent years, I have found myself alone, without my dear friends my age or family members. It's a bit unnerving to be advancing in my late 80's and not having the best people around. It was nice to know, though. I had one close friend still around who had known me for fifty years.

Our friendship began the day we both started at Charlotte Amalie High School. So yes, we know each other well. We were Guidance Counselors together in the same office. We went from the classroom to counseling. Even with the required qualifications, it would have been impossible for me to do as well as I did as a guidance counselor without her mentorship.

Dr. Tate and I now live a few miles from each other, and I want to share a few of her thoughts and comments:

"I have known Dr. White for over fifty years. I have seen her as an excellent counselor who is committed to her students and counselors. She has guided young people in personal and career activities. Many people who she worked with and influenced have achieved high levels in their personal lives and careers. Dr. White expanded her knowledge in many ways.

She participated in many venues. In addition to being a teacher and coordinator, Dr. White also holds a paralegal certificate from Adelphi University. She is regularly active in community, church, and statewide activities.

She performed well as Queen Guinevere at the Reichold Center in the play King Arthur. Her love for Pageantry at sixty-five years old started with me telling her, "Girl, I can't keep up with you." She cannot sit when her favorite music is playing. Ultimately, Dr. White loves people, and she works hard at being there for them, her family, friends, and community."

I do appreciate her comments so much. She has been my dear friend and my buddy throughout our fifty years of togetherness. To me, we're a dynamic force. We did so much together on many levels, both personal and professional. She didn't mention that we used to play Bid Whist at least fifty or more days each year for years and years. We laughed a lot about so many things, especially Bid Whist.

However, I'm peeved with her because even though we talked about being like the Golden Girls as we age, we didn't become those Golden Girls. We lived

Epilogue

our own version of them on the daily. Seriously though, we had great times together in our St. Thomas lifestyle. After Dr. Tate got her doctorate, I got mine because that, too, was "just logical. " It wasn't just for our good; to me, having my doctorate meant I could benefit my community.

Dr. Tate had always been there for me and would listen to me when I returned from wherever, like the United States, Hawaii, The Caribbean, Europe, and Dubai, to tell her about my travels. Often, if she couldn't get me on the phone, she assumed I was traveling somewhere. She'd always say to me, "Where are you now?" " I wished I was traveling, too."We just always had a lot to share.

In our lifetime, we often face unforeseen challenges to overcome. My perseverance and inner strength come from my favorite biblical verse: Proverbs 3:5-6: "Trust in the Lord with all your heart and lean not on your own understanding. In all your ways acknowledge Him and; He will direct your path!"

About the Author

Dr. Ida White is retired and a dedicated mother of two, retired Lutheran pastor Lester White, and retired Virgin Islands police corporal Denise White. Dr. White earned her BA in Social. Studies, her MA in Educational Administration, and her PhD in Counseling and Missiology Studies: She has two granddaughters, Jaimie and Lesli, and three great-grandchildren.

At 89 years young, Dr. White's journey began in New York City, where she was born and lived until she was 32 years old in 1967. At that point in her life, a voice or a sense of adventure encouraged her to take her family to a place where she knew hardly anyone, St. Thomas, US Virgin Islands, where she then spent 47 years blossoming in the Caribbean sun of St. Thomas, cultivating her own unique style and integrity.

Dr. White's illustrious career saw her retire from the employ of the Virgin Islands Department of Education on December 31, 1994. Yet, retirement was just the beginning. She brought her wisdom and experience to

FEMA, where she served as an Equal Rights Officer and Chief of Staff retiring at age 83. Dr. White discovered within her many "I can do that talents" and entered senior beauty pageants for 20 years and more, singing, dancing, expressing her comedic side, being in the award-winning film Pretty Old, and winning in 2022 a Global Beauty Award.

    Her commitment to community service is unwavering, from her active years and Rotary to her ongoing volunteer work in Kissimmee, Florida, where she currently lives. Dr. White's dedication to fostering global harmony is evident in her award of service as a Peace Ambassador to the UN. Her story is one of resilience, one of God at the center. Her focus is on learning, participating, and transforming in roles, no matter how small, to make the world a better place.

About the Author

SCAN ME

**Call or Text:
770-240-0089 Press Extension 1
Web: KLEpub.com
Email Services@klepub.com**

It's time to start and finish **YOUR Story!**

KLE Publishing specializes in helping people become authors. In as little as 15 to 90 days, we can help you develop your books and e-books and publish to 39,000 outlets! We also offer audiobook services.

Write, Edit, Format, Publis
We can help from
Start to Finish.

Explore and learn more about published authors affiliated with KLE.

KLEPub.com